THE REMARKABLE POTTERS OF SEAGROVE

THE FOLK POTTERY OF A LEGENDARY NORTH CAROLINA COMMUNITY

CHARLOTTE VESTAL BROWN

LARK BOOKS

A Division of Sterling Publishing Co., Inc.
New York

Editor: SUZANNE J. E. TOURTILLOTT

Art Director: DANA IRWIN

Cover Designer: BARBARA ZARETSKY

Associate Editor: NATHALIE MORNU

Associate Art Director: SHANNON YOKELEY

Assistant Art Director: LANCE WILLE

Art Production Assistant: JEFF HAMILTON

Editorial Assistance: DELORES GOSNELL,
DAWN DILLINGHAM

Editorial Interns: MEGAN TAYLOR COX,
SUE STIGLEMAN

Illustrators: BERNIE WOLF, *maps*
DANA IRWIN, *graphite drawings*

Photographer: TIM AYERS

Cover: BEN OWEN III, **Egg Vase**, 2000

Spine: ATTRIBUTED TO J. H. OWEN,
Four-Handled Floor Vase, circa 1920

Back: top row, left to right, J. B. COLE POTTERY,
Apothecary Jars, circa 1930s; GOTTFRIED AUST, **Slip-Decorated Plate**, circa 1780; BRUCE GHOLSON,
BULLDOG POTTERY, **Teapot with Fish**, 2002; AUMAN
POTTERY, **Basket**, circa 1927; ATTRIBUTED TO WAYMON
COLE, **Pair of Floor Vases**, circa 1940; UNKNOWN
POTTER FROM NORTHEASTERN UNITED STATES,
Shallow Dish, 1840–1850; center right, AUMAN
POTTERY-MASTEN collaboration, **Vase**, circa
1928–1930; bottom left, OSCAR L. BACHELDER,
Interior View of Omar Khayyam Pottery, 1927

Front flap: top, NELL COLE GRAVES; bottom, J. B.
COLE, **Elephant Pitcher**, circa 1930s

Back flap: top, WAYMON COLE;
bottom, ATTRIBUTED TO BEN OWEN OF JUGTOWN
POTTERY, left, **Grueby Jar**, right, **Lily Vase**,
both circa 1930s

Page 4: WAYMON COLE, **Urn**, 1984

Page 5: clockwise from top left,
AUMAN POTTERY-MASTEN collaboration, **Ovoid
Vase**, circa 1928–1930; J. B. COLE, **Pair of Trumpet
Vases**, circa 1930s; ATTRIBUTED TO BEN OWEN AT
JUGTOWN, **2 Persian Jars**, circa 1930–40, left,
12 x 16 inches (30.5 x 40.6 cm); right, 12 x 17 inches
(30.5 x 43.2 cm), Chinese blue salt glazed stoneware,
both stamped "Jugtown", collection of Gallery of Art &
Design, transfer from the North Carolina Museum of Art,
left, 1998.001.083, right, 1998.001.113;
BULLDOG POTTERY, **Vase**, 2004

Library of Congress Cataloging-in-Publication Data

Brown, Charlotte Vestal.
  The remarkable potters of Seagrove : the folk pottery of a legendary
North Carolina community / Charlotte Vestal Brown.-- 1st ed.
    p. cm.
  Includes bibliographical references and index.
  ISBN 1-57990-634-6 (hardcover)
  1. Pottery, American--North Carolina--Seagrove Region. 2. Folk art--
North Carolina--Seagrove Region. I. Title.
NK4027.S42B76 2006
738.309756'61--dc22

2006005522

10 9 8 7 6 5 4 3 2 1

First Edition

Published by Lark Books, A Division of
Sterling Publishing Co., Inc.
387 Park Avenue South, New York, N.Y. 10016

Text © 2006, Charlotte Vestal Brown
Photography © 2006, Lark Books unless otherwise specified
Illustrations © 2006, Lark Books unless otherwise specified

Distributed in Canada by Sterling Publishing,
c/o Canadian Manda Group, 165 Dufferin Street
Toronto, Ontario, Canada M6K 3H6

Distributed in the United Kingdom by GMC Distribution Services,
Castle Place, 166 High Street, Lewes, East Sussex, England BN7 1XU

Distributed in Australia by Capricorn Link (Australia) Pty Ltd.,
P.O. Box 704, Windsor, NSW 2756 Australia

If you have questions or comments about this book, please contact:
Lark Books, 67 Broadway, Asheville, NC 28801
(828) 253-0467

Manufactured in China

ISBN 13: 978-1-57990-634-4
ISBN 10: 1-57990-634-6

For information about custom editions, special sales, premium and
corporate purchases, please contact Sterling Special Sales Department at
800-805-5489 or specialsales@sterlingpub.com.

J. B. Cole unloading a groundhog kiln, circa 1920s.

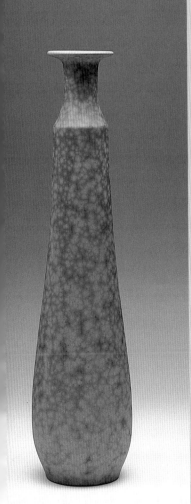

THE REMARKABLE POTTERS OF SEAGROVE

WRITING
SEAGROVE'S
HISTORY

WAYMON COLE, **Urn,** *1984*

Baxter Welch's pottery shop near Harper's Crossroads in Chatham County, circa 1900
COURTESY OF MR. AND MRS. GAILS WELCH

CHESTER WEBSTER, **Four-Gallon Syrup Jug,**
circa 1830–1840

T he potters working in the Seagrove area today have inherited the riches that only a long and successful tradition and a powerful sense of place can bestow on them. Pottery making has been an integral part of the lives of families there at least since the end of the 18th century. For a century or more, potters supplied the mostly utilitarian needs of their families and neighbors, who, like

THE POTTERY THEY MADE ENABLED PEOPLE TO SURVIVE. ITS FORMS, SHAPES, COLORS, AND TEXTURES EMBODIED THE PLACE, AS ITS MAKERS EMBEDDED THEIR VALUES IN THE WORK.

them, lived a fairly isolated, independent, subsistence farm life. The pottery they made enabled people to survive. Its forms, shapes, colors, and textures embodied the place, as its makers embedded their values in the work. These qualities were not deliberately self-conscious but rather the result of knowledge, practice, and the responsibility to make ware that functioned. When strictly utilitarian needs were supplanted by industrialization, making did not stop; the potters changed their work to accommodate new demands. And while forms, shapes, colors, and textures became more self-conscious, more diverse, and technically complex, survival continued to be a motivating force, as it is yet today.

Nell Cole Graves loading ware onto a drying shelf, circa 1920s. NORTH CAROLINA COLLECTION, UNIVERSITY OF NORTH CAROLINA LIBRARY AT CHAPEL HILL

View of the countryside near Seagrove from Daniel Johnston's kiln site.

The story of this craft's survival is one of an authentic and independent way of life. From self-reliance, tenacity, and persistence have come community and personal identity, forged by a job that has been both personally demanding and rewarding. This is a great story—nearly as attractive as the work itself. Today, close to 100 potteries produce ceramics within a 15-mile radius of Seagrove for a largely urbanized and mobile consumer society. Their patrons acquire ceramics for many different reasons, because the potters and many North Carolinians, whether native or new, live in a world where social and cultural changes have transformed handmade ceramics into symbols for many things: personal taste, status, and the pleasure of ownership being among the most important. As a North Carolinian, I have observed and experienced many of these changes during my lifetime.

The Seagrove area itself is still very beautiful; urbanization has been slow to arrive, although the landscape isn't as empty as it was 10 or 20 years ago. More homes line the roads, but people still have cattle and large gardens, and many continue to raise corn, wheat or tobacco, chickens or hogs, even though one or more family members may commute to jobs in nearby towns. People hold firmly to aspects of life that are traditional, especially in their attachment to the land. This is one of the reasons I wanted to write about the potters.

But above all I wanted to tell this story of survival. I'm convinced that the objects that people make embody their values, and the ceramics made in Seagrove over the past 200 years is one way to understand that story. Substantial archives and resources for understanding Seagrove's potters and their circumstances continue to grow, because we know that history—memories organized in some fashion—brings the past into the present, enriches and helps us to understand it, and sometimes gives us ideas about the future.

ATTRIBUTED TO BEN OWEN OF JUGTOWN POTTERY, **Egg Vases,** *circa 1930s*

Scholarship on the potters of the Seagrove area, in the form of publications and museum exhibitions, has flourished in the past 35 years. At the same time, the study of the history of craft in this country and region also has gained momentum. The North Carolina Pottery Center and the Museum of Traditional Pottery, both located in Seagrove itself, encourage exhibitions and still more research. Results of this academic inquiry are books like *North Carolina Pottery: The Collection of the Mint Museums* (University of North Carolina Press, 2004), edited by Barbara S. Perry. It is a serious scholarly documentation of that large collection, much of it from Dorothy and Walter Auman's collection assembled between about 1950 and 1991. Every publication or exhibition brings new perspectives on the subject at hand, and my narrative collects aspects of some of these perspectives in order to be able to focus specifically on a roughly 15-mile radius I have called, as folk scholar Georgeanna Greer did in 1981, the "Seagrove area." By their association with it, the potters themselves have defined this place. Their pottery is presented in the context of a changing North Carolina and the ways the potters have

Jacques and Juliana Busbee outside the Jugtown sales shop, about 1940.
COURTESY OF PAM AND VERNON OWENS, JUGTOWN

adapted to survive those changes. The first three chapters treat the history of the area from roughly 1800 to 2000, and the final chapter focuses on Seagrove today, including highlights about several of its most intriguing contemporary makers and their amazing work.

Seagrove's continued and successful integration of clay as a part of daily life is comparable to such unique pottery centers as France's La Borne and the Japanese village of Shigaraki. The Seagrove area is just as remarkable—both as a place and a state of mind.

CHAPTER I

SEAGROVE'S ROOTS

"The mysterious Uwharries are very beautiful. It is said of Randolph that it is one county where every road is a scenic highway…

"This combination of woods, of numerous streams, rolling hills swelling into mountain knobs and ridges all interspersed by occasional wide open lands…makes Randolph an exceedingly attractive section." [1]

J. D. Craven,
Five-Gallon Jug,
circa 1890

Edward Webster,
One-Gallon Jug,
circa 1825

The white settlers who brought pottery making to the wooded hills and open savannahs of North Carolina's Piedmont counties began to arrive in the second half of the 18th century. This slow stream of people rolled down the Great Wagon Road from Philadelphia, coming south to the Catawba Valley, just west of Seagrove by about 100 miles, or they came via the Trading Path that ran south and west from Petersburg, Virginia.

These immigrants might have thought the land was beautiful but they also knew it would be hard going as they encountered rolling hills, thick stands of trees, shallow creeks and rivers, rocky paths and outcroppings, and a dense soil rich in iron, mica, and red, brown, tan, and yellow clay. But they were undaunted by the terrain; they were in search of cheap or even free land where they could farm and raise their families and lead lives according to their own lights.

The German, Scots-Irish, Welsh, and English settlers had relocated before, and just as before, they brought their traditions with them. Many kept their ties with the families they had left behind in the Northeast and mid-Atlantic states. They also brought a diversity of religions. Quakers, Baptists, Lutherans, Moravians, Methodists, and Dunkers filled in the empty spaces and soon gave the area a particular flavor—one of individualism and equality. George Seolle, a Moravian missionary who visited northern Randolph County in 1771, wrote, "They have Moravian, Quaker, Separatist, Dunkard principles, know everything and know nothing, look down on others, belong to no one, and spurn others."[2]

In the near middle of the Piedmont plateau, with the state capitol of Raleigh (founded in 1792) to the east, the Uwharrie Mountains to the west, and Cross Creek (later to be renamed Fayetteville) to the southeast, the settlers carved out many new counties. Pottery was made in eight of these counties during the 19th century, but by the end of that period, four dominated: Chatham, Moore, Montgomery, and Randolph. In the three latter counties, production clustered in a rough 15-mile radius where the three came together near the road that ran from Cross Creek northeast toward the Moravian settlements in Forsyth County. In time, county seats, churches, courthouses, and dwellings were built, along with a few roads.

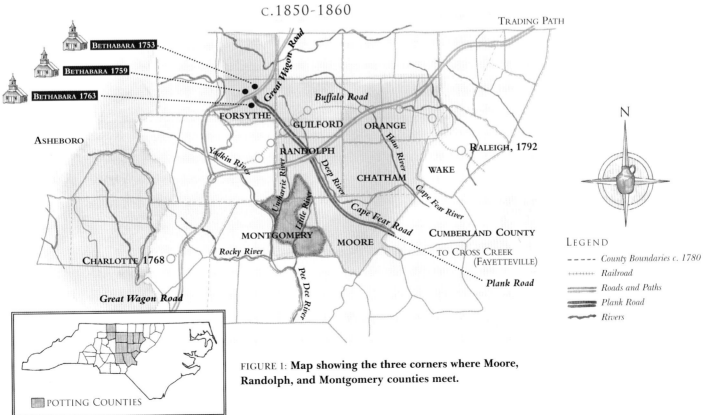

19TH-CENTURY PIEDMONT NORTH CAROLINA
c. 1850-1860

FIGURE 1: **Map showing the three corners where Moore, Randolph, and Montgomery counties meet.**

PHOTO 1: UNKNOWN QUAKER FAMILY, **Grandmother's Choice or Pinwheel "Signature" Quilt**, *1880–1910. 86 x 72 inches (218.4 x 182.9 cm). Machine-pieced cotton, feed sacking, hand quilted; embroidered signatures in each block include the names Craven, Hancock, and Shelton. Collection of Gallery of Art & Design, North Carolina State University, Patty Royster James Quilt Collection, gift of Everette James and Nancy Farmer, 2000.031.026*

PHOTO 2: ENOCH SPINKS CRAVEN, **Storage or Canning Jar**, *mid 19th century. Height, 6¾ x 5½ inches (17.1 x 14 cm). Salt-glazed stoneware; stamped "E S Craven". Collection of Gallery of Art & Design, North Carolina State University, gift of Ray Wilkinson, 2001.001.005*

River access was limited by the waterfalls along the line where the Piedmont plateau rises above the coastal plain. Only small, shallow boats could navigate the rivers and creeks. These conditions meant that the counties experienced a long period of relative isolation from the rest of the state (figure 1, page 11).

THE RURAL LIFE

Like many pioneers, these settlers often were skilled at one or more trades; there were coopers and carpenters, harness makers and tailors, seamstresses and millers, preachers and brick masons, blacksmiths, teachers, and potters. Yet these immigrants were unlike the Anglicans and Presbyterians who had dominated North Carolina's rich coastal plain since the early 18th century. There, slaves farmed cash crops of cotton, indigo, and tobacco, and harvested the stands of pines for tar, pitch, and turpentine. These settlers considered themselves landed gentry, and their social customs and attitudes toward others were founded on the wealth their holdings produced. Their faith incorporated a hierarchical system of class that was reflected in practices like boxed pews for certain families. Their crops were traded with Europe via the Caribbean routes, and they bought furniture, textiles, and ceramics from abroad and from places like Baltimore, Philadelphia, and New York. They believed in their own importance and their "right" to great political power in the state.

In contrast, the Piedmont's agricultural production and its forest resources were utilized only for the support of the farmers. Until sufficient transportation networks existed to move and sell crops and harvest timber, there was no incentive to grow more than was needed. Moreover, the Piedmont settlers brought to North Carolina their dissenting religions' resistance to slavery. Abolitionist sentiment was especially strong among the Quakers and some Methodist congregations. At their yearly meeting of 1776, Quakers were admonished to "cleanse their hands of slaves as soon as they possibly can."[3]

As the coastal plantations grew increasingly prosperous, their owners accumulated wealth and political power that they did not want to share with the growing population in the Piedmont.

Although the falls along the rivers could provide water power to generate the energy required for industry, the eastern politicians opposed roads and dams. The Piedmont counties were considered the "backcountry," a pejorative term that referred not only to the geographic isolation of the area, but also to most of the settlers' smaller holdings, lesser income, and undoubtedly lower-class origins. Backcountry also implied a lack of education, and in time came to mean a distrust of outsiders and a fierce individuality that sometimes resulted in inflexible attitudes and behavior. Backcountry families looked to each other and to their neighbors for support as communities and congregations struggled, endured, then conquered the hard frontier life. First houses and churches were usually log cabins that expanded and improved as time and income permitted. Their craftsmen provided families and businesses with distinctive pottery, textiles, and furniture. "Neat and plain" were common descriptions in contracts and requests to suppliers. Their houses, churches, furniture, quilts, and ceramics (photos 1 and 2) were shaped by the materials and conditions the settlers found in the new land, and by the values of thrift, modesty, and simplicity that were associated with their religious beliefs. German and English ways provided models and traditions, and the climate and the land shaped the work profoundly.

In the Seagrove area, the farmers' self-reliance grew from their backbreaking labor, as they cleared the forested and sometimes rocky land to make fields for planting and grazing. Townships were established: New Salem, Pleasant Grove, and Trinity in Randolph County. Villages appeared with names like Erect, Hemp, Lonely, Sofia, Steeds, and Whynot. They put up churches—at least 40 in Randolph County by the end of the 19th century, while Moore claimed about the same number by 1898.

The lush green landscape, its gently rolling swales and fields drained by the Deep, the Haw, the Uwharrie, and the Little rivers and their numerous creeks and tributaries, presented a variety of resources for new settlers. In northern Randolph County, for example, the dense clay soil was used for pastures, fields, gardens, and pottery, while the Sandhills region to the south, with its deep, sandy soil and long-leafed pine forests, was good for

PHOTO 3: ATTRIBUTED TO THE COLE FAMILY, **Two-Handled Storage Jar**, *circa 1880. 12½ x 10 inches (30.5 x 25.4 cm). Salt-glazed stoneware; stamped "3" under handle. Collection of Gallery of Art & Design, North Carolina State University, gift of the Friends of the Gallery Collectors Circle, 2005.012.002*

timber and turpentine. Waterfalls, rushing down from the Uwharrie Mountains into the Deep River, encouraged milling. Near Asheboro, Moore's county seat, Quaker investors built two of North Carolina's first pre-Civil War textile mills. In 1849, the Fayetteville and Western Plank Road opened.

The Plank Road, 129 miles long, continued to Asheboro and Salem in Forsyth County. As a convenient and direct connection to urban markets

both north and south, the Plank Road "opened up rural Randolph like nothing else prior to the railroads of the 1880s."[4] But the road was expensive and hard to maintain, and during the Civil War years it fell apart. Later, the North Carolina Railroad partially replaced it, and eventually smaller start-up rail lines with names like Aberdeen & Asheboro were joined to it.

Pottery was crucial for pioneering families; they needed stew pots, pans, dinnerware, churns, jars, and bottles to prepare, serve, and store food (photo 3, page 13). Jugs in many sizes held honey, molasses, liquor, and vinegar. Household goods also included a variety of other items: baking dishes, colanders (photo 4), candlesticks and lanterns, chamber pots and washbasins, whistles and smoking pipes, even gravestones, water pipes, drain tiles, and flues—all were made of clay (photo 5).

Rural life followed daily and seasonal patterns, and revolved around planting and harvest, the daylight and dark, the moderate winters and hot, humid summers of the Piedmont. Births, deaths, weddings, and church- and community-related events linked the families and enlivened and elevated the quality of community life.

WAR AND BEYOND

When the Civil War erupted, the anti-slavery factions of the Piedmont, including Randolph County, were heavily Unionist, and Governor Vance sent troops to put down anti-Confederate disturbances. Potters were exempt from recruitment because the wares they made were considered essential to the war effort. The traditionally named Confederate cup or beaker was just one of the many items (like bowls and dirt dishes) used by the rebel soldiers in the field; storage jars were needed to hold preserved foodstuffs, water, molasses, beer, and liquor (photo 6).

The end of the war brought profound changes, especially in the transformation of North Carolina's economic system. A vigorous period of industrialization brought wealth and political power to the Piedmont, including the counties surrounding Seagrove. An unknown potter, jubilant at the election of Jonathan Worth, a Randolph native and a Republican, made a political pot that proclaimed, "Jo'han, Jo'han/Jo'han Worth/Run, Run for all Your Worth Hurrah

Hurrah for Jo'han Worth."[5] As industrialization and manufacturing spread, small mill towns grew. Railroads moved deep into the fresh territory, moving out timber in order to supply the railroad, the building-supply industry, and furniture manufacturing.

The postwar years were also a period of grief and acrimony among friends and families sundered by the war. The decline and decay of property, whether through neglect, vandalism, or theft, was significant. Schools were abandoned, cattle killed and lost. All areas of North Carolina struggled to recover from the war's devastation. Until farms could be restored to their former levels of productivity, poverty and hunger were familiar to all. Eventually, though, the recovery that swept the state affected even the potters in the Seagrove area. Making pottery was a source of income and pride to them.

EARLY POTTERY IN THE PIEDMONT

Pottery and the knowledge to make it came down the wagon roads with the people who moved to the Piedmont. Potters used what they knew and adapted themselves and their wares to the conditions they found, and created a pottery particular to their new home, a pottery that would become the traditional, vernacular pottery of the 19th century.

PHOTO 7: UNKNOWN POTTER FROM NORTHEASTERN UNITED STATES, **Shallow Dish**, *1840–1850. 2½ x 8 inches (6.4 x 20.3 cm). Earthenware; yellow slip decoration; lead glaze. Collection of Gallery of Art & Design, North Carolina State University, gift of the Friends of the Gallery Collectors Circle, 1999.024.002*

PHOTO 6: UNKNOWN PIEDMONT POTTER, **Rebel Dirt Dish**, *circa 1863–1864. 1½ x 8½ inches (3.8 x 21.6 cm). Stoneware; painted inscription around well reads "Rebel crockery Manufactured during the blockade of our Southern Coast, Captured Charlotte NC Apl 1865w/Confederate Medical Stores stampeding from Richmond JWP USSG/Used So. Military Hospital." Mint Museum of Art, Charlotte, North Carolina. Museum Purchase. H1985.57*

Almost certainly, all the settlers were familiar with the three kinds of clay bodies: earthenware, stoneware, and porcelain. Earthenware, sometimes called redware (a name derived from the predominant color of its clay), was made all over the Eastern Seaboard, wherever the clay could be found. Redware was only replaced when prosperity and industrialization made it obsolete. The shallow dish in photo 7 has some of the most endearing characteristics of earthenware. Its rich color under the clear lead glaze and a contrasting color of decoration derived from a thin, watery slip that was painted on before the piece was fired are appealing. The decoration is lively, the dish is lightweight, and it shows the hand of its maker. Some of the problems of earthenware are evident, too: its surface is worn and chipped, the glaze has rubbed off, and the clay body shows through the worn glaze like the frayed edge of a shirt cuff. Earthenware also cracks easily, and it can leak or hold food deposits in the cracks. Only its decoration probably saved this piece from being tossed out.

PHOTO 8: UNKNOWN ROCKBRIDGE COUNTY, VIRGINIA POTTER, **Two-Handled Storage Jar**, *mid 19th century. 10 x 7 inches (25.4 x 17.8 cm). Salt-glazed stoneware; cobalt decoration. Collection of Gallery of Art & Design, North Carolina State University, estate of George Needham, 2005.012.001*

Stoneware, usually salt glazed, was a common utilitarian ware that was probably first made in Germany then came to the British Isles during the Renaissance. Immigrant production potters in the Northeast and mid-Atlantic states produced it in the 18th and 19th centuries. A mid-19th century, two-handled storage jar (photo 8) from

PHOTO 9: UNKNOWN CHINESE POTTERS, **Blue-and-White Export Ware (also called Canton Ware) Candlesticks, Cup, and Saucer**, *mid 19th century. Candlesticks: 7¾ inches (19.7 cm) high; cup: 2¼ x 3½ inches (5.7 x 8.9 cm); saucer: 5½ inches (14 cm) in diameter. Porcelain; hand-painted cobalt decoration. Collection of Gallery of Art & Design, North Carolina State University, estate of George Needham, (candlesticks) 1994.019.006a, b; (cup and saucer) 1994.019.093b, d*

Rockbridge County, Virginia, has the cool gray surface that is characteristic of stoneware. Its lively, freehand cobalt decoration, applied before the pot was fired, looks like holiday swags of leaves and berries. Stoneware can be fired to a higher temperature than earthenware, so that the clay actually vitrifies. The result is a stronger, more durable clay body that is especially suited to large jars, such as churns and storage vessels, because it can sustain repeated hard use.

Porcelain, the finest ceramic ware made in Asia and Europe, was imported to America, where it graced the homes of the wealthy. Blue-and-white export ware made in China was as popular in this country as European porcelains (photo 9). The time, effort, and expense required to fashion, decorate, and fire the kaolin-rich clay put porcelain out of reach for potter and buyer alike, and so, in central North Carolina, practical and utilitarian earthenware and stoneware became the kinds of ceramics most in demand (photo 10).

The Moravians, a German-based Christian sect that emigrated from Pennsylvania to Forsyth County (in the upper Piedmont) in the middle of the 18th century, brought their earthenware tradition to North Carolina. In less than a single generation, they founded the towns of Bethabara, Bethania, and, in 1766, Salem, "a planned congregational and trading center."[6] Soon the settlements were firmly entrenched in a closed, agrarian economy, where the Brethren lived in a church-governed religious society.

In the 1770s, Moravian master potter Gottfried Aust held a sale in his Bethabara shop. Records tell of "an unusual concourse of visitors, some coming 60 or 80 miles, to buy milk crocks and pans in our pottery. They bought the entire stock, not one piece was left; many could only get half what they wanted, and others, who came too late, could find none."[7]

Glazed and decorated Moravian earthenware was the sophisticated fruit of long European tradition. Such wares were either thrown or molded, and the attention to design and execution is evident in all that the Moravian potters made, whether beautiful ceremonial pieces or utilitarian ware created for daily use (photo 11).

Such earthenware was made from red clay dug at or just below the ground's surface and, in the

18th and 19th centuries, fired in a wood-fueled kiln. Two firings were required, the first at a relatively low temperature, which required less fuel and labor but resulted in relatively fragile bisque-ware. After the application of decorative motifs and glaze, it was fired a second time to temperatures that reached 1800°F (982.2°C), resulting in a more durable and glasslike surface. Earthenware for the kitchen was also made in the Seagrove area. Its typically clear, lead-based glazes were easy to make and fire. Such formulations produced strong, bright colors, but even in the early 19th century people realized lead was a dangerous substance. Although Moravians knew of salt-glazed stoneware from the northeast and from Germany, and they experimented with it, stoneware did not replace their earthenware. However, by early in the 19th century, salt-glazed stoneware probably joined the earthenware that was already in common use in Seagrove.

USING THE LAND

The Piedmont is blessed with all kinds of clay. A freshly plowed field, red or yellow or orange in the spring sun, falling away to a clear blue sky at the horizon, sings to the native a song of sticky-bottomed shoes and recalcitrant soil that colors clothes permanently—and yet sustains crops and cattle. While local earthenware was made from surface clay, stoneware was made from the local clay seams that were found along creek banks, river bottoms, or pits below grade. The potter and whatever help was at hand had to laboriously dig out this deeper clay (photo 12, page 18). Because it had been formed differently than surface clay, it was a slicker, leaner, and cleaner clay. Today, stoneware potters say "the deeper the better."

A freshly plowed field of red clay may be a gorgeous color, but it is also a tumble of stony knots, clumps, and clots of clay. And no matter whether surface or deeper dug, the biggest rocks, sticks, weeds, leaves, and other debris had to first be removed. Then the newly dug clay was ground (or "pugged"), dried, and re-wet, and otherwise fussed over in a labor-intensive process that, depending on weather conditions and relative humidity, could take days or weeks. When the clay was malleable enough, it was vigorously wedged to eliminate air pockets that would otherwise cause pots to explode in the kiln. The clay was

PHOTO 10: Unknown Seagrove-area potter, **Slip-Decorated Plate**, *circa 1800–1825. 2 x 11 inches (5.1 x 27.9 cm). Lead-glazed earthenware; slip decoration. Mint Museum of Art, Charlotte, North Carolina. Gift of the Mint Museum Auxiliary and Daisy Wade Bridges from the Collection of Walter and Dorothy Auman. H1983.190.25*

PHOTO 11: Gottfried Aust, **Slip-Decorated Plate**, *circa 1780. 2½ x 11¼ inches (6.4 x 28.6 cm). Earthenware; slip decoration. Mint Museum of Art, Charlotte, North Carolina. Gift of the Mint Museum Auxiliary and Daisy Wade Bridges from the Collection of Walter and Dorothy Auman. H1983.190.39*

PHOTO 12: **Baxter Welch pottery workers digging stoneware clay in Chatham County, circa 1900**
COURTESY OF MR. AND MRS. GAILS WELCH

 A FRESHLY PLOWED FIELD OF RED CLAY MAY BE A GORGEOUS COLOR, BUT IT IS ALSO A TUMBLE OF STONY KNOTS, CLUMPS, AND CLOTS OF CLAY.

then stored and allowed to season and seep water. Finally, the clay was divided into jar-, cup-, bowl-, or gallon-sized lumps for the potter to throw on the wheel. Experience, handed from father to son or potter to potter, quickly trained them to recognize exactly how much clay was needed for each specific use. But before a single piece could be thrown, the potter had to construct a kiln and get his firing wood ready. Fortunately, in the Seagrove area, wood was plentiful.

Many early potters used their first clay to make kiln bricks fired with wood in a pit dug in the ground. The cross-draft kiln popular in 19th-century North Carolina was first developed in China some 2000 years ago. As the design moved westward, it shaped the European rectangular kiln, which had been developed in Germany by the 15th century. It was finally adapted in America so that it could be fired by a single potter, his family, and maybe some friends. The aptly named (because it resembles a burrowing animal)

groundhog kiln is a long, low, arched tunnel or flue set into the ground with a firebox at one end and a wide chimney at the other (figure 2). The side-loading beehive design, a round kiln with a central chimney that was fired underneath the floor, may have been used as well, but the front-loading groundhog kiln became the preferred design. It was reliable, dependable, rough, and ready for steady use; it was easy to repair the structure when its bricks began to sag or fall in along the spine.

The potter threw pots while standing or sitting at his kick or treadle wheel, kicking or pumping it with his leg hundreds of times a day (photo 13). A potter might turn 50 to 100 pieces a day—or more, depending on his skill, energy, and concentration. The pieces were left to dry in a shed the potter had constructed for that purpose. If earthenware, two firings were needed. Stoneware, however, was fired only once, which may be another reason for its widespread use. The ware

FIGURE 2: **Groundhog kiln. The firebox is inside the entrance and below the shelf or floor where the ware is placed for firing.**

was "salted" (i.e., salt thrown into the kiln) during the last part of the firing, when it vaporized in the tremendous heat and combined with the silica in the clay body to produce a glazed surface on the ware. Salt may have been adopted because it is the simplest way to create a vitreous coating on ceramic ware; other types of ceramic (non-salted) ware often require a second, or glaze, firing.

There is plenty of evidence that earthenware was common in the Seagrove area in the 19th century, but sturdy salt-glazed stoneware has more successfully survived the ensuing years. The widespread presence of the clay that was ideal for high firing was eventually discovered by potters who recognized the clay's potential through trial and experiment. The stoneware practice (i.e., how to fire and glaze it) could have first come to Seagrove from any of the earliest immigrant groups.

High-fired clay enabled the Seagrove potters to make functional ware that had great strength, and that resisted cracking and separating. In retrospect, stoneware also has its own intrinsic beauty, although its aesthetic quality can't be definitively attributed to the potters themselves. Until the

PHOTO 13: **Early potter's wheel with wooden ribs (for shaping ware) on window frame. The "head" of the wheel is turned by the larger, heavy kick wheel below the potter's seat (note depression in long board).**

PHOTO 14: ENOCH SPRINKS CRAVEN, **Jug**, *circa 1850.*
12 x 7 inches (30.5 x 17.8 cm). Salt-glazed stoneware; "E.
S. Craven" impressed on shoulder. Mint Museum of Art,
Charlotte, North Carolina. Gift of the Mint Museum
Auxiliary and Daisy Wade Bridges from the Collection of
Walter and Dorothy Auman. H1983.190.75

20th century, wood was the only fuel available to fire a kiln. Fortunately, the local clay was well suited to the plentiful fuel.

Wood firing, while a dramatic and exciting event, is full of opportunity for disaster. The potter and any helpers he could muster loaded the fragile, bone-dry pots into the kiln through a low opening. The potter dragged the ware, set upon a board, with him as he moved to the back of the kiln, where the chimney rises. The pots were carefully removed from the board and arranged on flints, sand, or pebbles. He filled the kiln from the chimney end to the front, where the firebox sits below grade. An experienced potter knew how to pack the kiln to take best advantage of the limited space. Sometimes the ware was stacked, but usually it was lined up on the level surface of the kiln floor (sometimes called a shelf), with the tallest pieces in the center. A small fire was kindled in the firebox and the temperature brought up slowly to be sure all the pots were dry and to avoid exploding or cracking from thermal shock. When judged warm enough by the potter, the kiln's opening was partially closed. Some potters bricked it shut; others used a metal hatch or cover, but an opening had to be left to permit feeding the firebox.

To reach the necessary 2300°F–2400°F (1260°C–1315.5°C) for salt glazing, the potter had to create a pyrotechnical kiln condition called blasting off. Near the end of the firing period, the fire was stoked faster and faster with resinous pine wood (the resins generated great heat). As sheets of flame erupted from the chimney, clumps of salt were tossed into kiln ports. The high heat vaporized the salt, and this vapor united with silica in the clay body to create a glaze. Ash from the burning wood, flying through the kiln, landed on the pots' shoulders and created drips and runs on their sides; uneven heat caused flashes of darker and lighter colors. Accretions of salt and ash, dripping from the kiln's ceiling, dotted the pots below. Tiny rocks left in the clay sometimes cracked a surface or gently protruded from it.

All these firing "accidents" contributed to the individuality and the distinctive appearance of the pots, and some that emerged from the intense process can only be described as beautiful. Enoch

S. Craven's 19th-century jug (photo 14) has great ash deposits on one side. The incised rings above the shoulder capture these runs, making a strong contrast between darker and lighter circles. The drips that run over the pot's shoulder emphasize its slightly bumpy yet seemingly oily surface. Craven's skillful piece demonstrates that he knew what he could expect from his kiln.

Once the blast off was finished, the heat was allowed to diminish slowly (again, to avoid thermal shock) so that the kiln could cool down over the next day or two. Only when the kiln was unloaded did the potter learn the results of his tremendous labor. Yet there was still more work to be done. The pots were set out on the ground, damaged ones discarded; pebbles or flints, fused to the bottoms, were knocked away and the bottoms sanded even, so the pots could stand firmly on the earth, in a cold creek, or on the wooden floor of a cabin. When a firing was finished, the kiln needed maintenance, then the process started over again.

Potting, like farming, was seasonal. As harvest time neared, more ceramics were needed for food preservation, so after spring planting and also the late summer, into autumn, were good times for potting work, when more daylight made even more work possible. The potter's crop—storage jars and churns, milk crocks and bottles, or earthenware plates, mugs and bowls—might be peddled from a wagon bed or sold from the potter's own shop. Meanwhile, the other work of the family continued alongside the heavy labor of pottery making. At a time when all the roads were dirt (and some not so much road as track or rutted path), proximity was valuable to both maker and buyer. By the middle of the century, ceramic work was also acquired by wholesale merchants who intended to sell the wares in town or to distillers of whiskey and makers of molasses and other bottled goods.

At every step within the strict, demanding framework of throwing and firing were infinite possibilities for creative exploration. The potter could alter the process in some minute or large way, and each alteration might not only literally reshape the outcome but also expand the degree of the unpredictable. This mutability challenged and engaged the potter on a daily basis. He worked within a predictable pattern of tradition, which had a high practical value, and the unpredictable, which was stimulating.

The potter was a maker with skills and knowledge that he acquired through much practical experience, which could be shared and passed on to still other potters. With such a wealth of useful experience, he could work for generations with great confidence and freedom. Ultimately, these values were transferred to the work itself, marrying tradition to personal skill and making ceramics of value, both for the potter and the community.

EARLY STONEWARE

No one knows for sure who the first potter was to set up shop in the Seagrove area. Oral history has long held that 18th-century resident Peter Craven, an English immigrant, was Seagrove's earliest potter, but that is unlikely. Peter's grandson, John Craven, died in 1832, and he was definitely a potter; his estate's inventory lists "1 poters [sic] wheel and crank."[8] John fathered one of Seagrove's potting dynasties, and his descendants took potting to Georgia, Tennessee, and Missouri, but some

FIRING "ACCIDENTS" CONTRIBUTED TO THE INDIVIDUALITY AND THE DISTINCTIVE APPEARANCE OF THE POTS

family members remain in Randolph County to this day. One of John's sons, Anderson Craven, fathered four sons, of whom three were potters: John A., Thomas W., and Jacob Dorris (J. D.), one of the most successful of the area's 19th-century potters, who made fine salt-glazed stoneware.

By 1820, salt-glazed stoneware, made at the firm of Gurdon Robins and Company in Fayetteville (formerly named Cross Creek), was available in this part of North Carolina. Robins was from Hartford, Connecticut, and his company also "imported" earthenware and stoneware from Philadelphia, Boston, Rhode Island, and New York, as well as from England and the Caribbean. Encouraged by sales, Robins hired a potter,

Edward Webster, a member of a prominent family of Hartford potters. Robins was not successful in selling the stoneware Webster made at Robins' shop, although he advertised it as cheaper and comparable in quality to the American as well as other "imported" ceramic wares. When Robins' business closed, Edward Webster and his brothers Chester and Timothy moved farther northwest, into the area around Seagrove. Why the Websters left Hartford to move south and work for Robins is a mystery, but why they stayed on in the Piedmont of North Carolina is easier to guess: they found an opportunity to make pottery; they found a home.

By the mid 1850s, handmade utilitarian pottery in the Northeast and in Maryland and Virginia was already being replaced by factory-made ware. The full transition took several generations, but in the Piedmont, both the lower income of many

PHOTO 15: EDWARD WEBSTER, **One-Gallon Jug**, *circa 1825. Height, 12½ inches (31.8 cm). Stoneware; stamped "Edward Webster/Fayetteville". Mint Museum of Art, Charlotte, North Carolina. Gift of the Mint Museum Auxiliary and Daisy Wade Bridges from the Collection of Walter and Dorothy Auman. H1983.190.17*

farmers and the small communities' and farms' continued dependence on mostly local resources provided opportunities for a family like the Websters to continue their skilled work and to thrive at it. They achieved a measure of respect as artisans that was diminishing in other parts of the country as industrialization expanded. Craft, talent, and skill ensured a recognized role in a community; the potters were just as valuable to the community as doctors, preachers, teachers, midwives, or weavers.

The Websters brought a more refined and sophisticated pottery language to Randolph County. Edward Webster made this fine jug about 1825 (photo 15). It is stamped "Edward Webster/Fayetteville" on the shoulder opposite the handle. The brown color derives from an iron wash applied beneath the salt glaze. The high shoulder, belly and narrow base were more traditional in the Northeast, his home. Edward eventually left the state, but his brother, Chester, remained and left a large body of work.

Chester worked for Solomon, then B. Y. Craven in Randolph County, and he produced some of the area's most beautiful surviving ware, sometimes decorated with incised foliage, birds, fish, geometric borders and banding. Chester's stoneware probably influenced other local makers who observed his refinements. His forms have tight, crisp bodies and firm, elegant profiles that never waver. Openings are exactly the right size for each piece. Handles are carefully shaped to fit the hand, and the bodies are well balanced, neither top or bottom heavy. The prickly fish (photo 16) seems placed to emphasize the shoulder of the vessel, to "swim" above the pot's belly. As Chester's work matured, he combined his particular style with the local salt-glazed stoneware, which enriched both his work and that of subsequent potters.

Manufacturing Stoneware

J. D. Craven, Anderson Craven's middle son, moved to Moore County near the present site of the Jugtown Pottery between 1850 and 1860, perhaps because of family tensions over slavery but probably also because there were no potters living there at that time. Craven's site was located on the newly completed Plank Road that ran from Fayetteville to Asheboro and beyond. Such easy access made the area a logical place to set up shop. Craven was not alone for long, because other potters soon came to the area.

In the 1860 Manufacturers' Census, J. D. Craven was described as a "mannufactor of stoneware," who employed "three men to use 60,000 pounds of clay, 16 bushels of salt, and 20 cords of wood to make 6,000 gallons of jugs, churns, crocks, and pitchers valued at $600." That's a penny a gallon. Ten years later, his shop worked seven months of the year and employed four potters. Two of them, W. H. Hancock, age 26, and Henry Luck, 23, lived next to the Craven home. J. D. had turned a home pottery into an industry with an output clearly intended for more than a local market. Many pieces were being sold to wholesalers or manufacturers and providing Craven and his employees stable sources of income. His stamped pieces established him as an immensely prolific producer (photo 17, page 24).

The young potters who worked for Craven trained alongside his sons, Daniel and Isaac, who also had their own shops. In addition to Hancock and Luck, Benjamin Franklin Owen and William H. Chrisco also worked with J. D.; these surnames remained associated with Seagrove-area pottery production well into the 20th century. These were the last generation of true folk potters, who produced only handmade and wood-fired functional ware using the methods and forms that they had learned from their families. These wares were built on a work ethic of self-sufficiency and adherence to tried-and-true methods of working that almost always succeeded. Chance effects inherent in the organic clay and its response to both the firing and to the kiln itself enriched their work so much that while their methods stayed fairly consistent, the work of individual potters was still recognizable (photo 18, page 25). When J. D.'s grandsons, C. B. and Ferrell, matured in the next century, these traditional skills and methods enabled them to contribute to the evolution of the folk pottery tradition just as it was being threatened by the transformation of North Carolina's liquor laws and by changing tastes.

Personal tastes and a pottery shopping trip were described in an 1876 visit to Evan Cole's pottery near Whynot. Evan was part of the Cole potting dynasty that was very active during this period. This account includes reference to his ancestor,

Aunt Rebecca W., who wrote to her niece, Anne: "I went with Rossinah…to get somethings for setting in her house making. They are distant kin to us by Aunt Rach that you never knew but herd us talk of was Mark's wife. Sallie was airing bedding and showed us one of old Aunt Rach covers that was so fine work but

PHOTO 16: CHESTER WEBSTER, **Four-Gallon Syrup Jug**, *circa 1830–1840. Height, 18 inches (45.7 cm). Brown salt-glazed stoneware; "4" incised at neck, fish incised on shoulder. Mint Museum of Art, Charlotte, North Carolina. Gift of the Mint Museum Auxiliary and Daisy Wade Bridges from the Collection of Walter and Dorothy Auman. H1983.190.34*

PHOTO 17: J. D. CRAVEN, **Five-Gallon Jug**, *circa 1890. 22 x 9 inches (55.9 x 22.9 cm). Salt-glazed stoneware, stamped "5".*
PHOTO BY TIM AYERS, COLLECTION OF NORTH CAROLINA POTTERY CENTER

old and worn and not in use for it covered Rafe [Cole] when he passed. Rossinah got a stone churn and milk pans and pie dishes and saw a teapot but did not buy that. I got you a cake mole with blue decoration since you admired mine so long. Hope you like it well."[9] On the way home, they got stuck in the mud but they had a good trip.

J. D. Craven was not the only mannufactor. The post–Civil War Piedmont saw broad expansions in manufacturing, transportation, and communication. The state's residents had to make what they needed, and potters could certainly do that as well as spinners, weavers, and manufacturers of tobacco products, building supplies, and furniture. With the exception of pottery production, all of these industries encouraged the relocation of people and materials from the countryside to towns. Naturally, industry promoted acceptance of the "newness" of manufactured products, which in turn spurred the development of a consumer society.

The communities in the Seagrove area remained firmly agricultural long after the Civil War, until the cacophony of growth, with its concomitant changes in farming and a declining way of life for the potters, took its toll. The number of farms began to diminish. Beginning in the middle 1880s, the Piedmont's small, independent, and usually self-supporting farmers turned more and more to cash-crop farming, which in turn made them ever more reliant on a cash-based consumer economy. At about this time, farmers were encouraged to turn feed corn (formerly raised for cattle) into whiskey and potters to produce jugs for those who made the corn liquor. Farming as an occupation suffered, and younger family members began to move to the growing towns and cities because manufacturing jobs offered a predictable income. Life in towns with stores, bars, and more people was exciting. Yet salt-glazed stoneware production remained steady in the Seagrove area, and it sometimes achieved an extraordinary level of quality. Domestic and retail use of ceramics, the two major markets, continued, in spite of the new society that was slowly emerging.

In 1884, a group of entrepreneurs from Raleigh, Salem, and other North Carolina cities successfully developed an exposition to celebrate the state's progress since the war's end. At the opening cere-

IN 1860, J. D. CRAVEN EMPLOYED THREE MEN TO USE 60,000 POUNDS OF CLAY, 16 BUSHELS OF SALT, AND 20 CORDS OF WOOD TO MAKE 6,000 GALLONS OF JUGS, CHURNS, CROCKS, AND PITCHERS

monies, Governor Thomas Jarvis proclaimed that "Today, North Carolinians have discovered North Carolina." Agriculture and education were represented along with entertainment in music, minstrels, and games of chance, but the exposition focused mainly on industry.

The temporary exposition hall (photo 19, page 26), as well as its displays, was symbolic of the advancement of the state's industries. The structure was erected by the North Carolina Car Company, who specialized in making prefabricated building components. The lumber was brought by a special train spur line from Blue's Crossing in Moore County. The exposition demonstrated the ability to succeed and it inspired hope.

The exposition was a spur to effort in many ways. Some of the impetus that created the exposition translated into the founding of the College of Agricultural and Mechanical Arts in Raleigh. With funds provided by the federal land grant Morrill Act, the A and M, as it came to be called, opened its doors in 1889. The school was committed to improving the lives of the citizens of the state, and one of the first departments created was ceramics engineering, inspired in part by the history of the state's indigenous production.

SEAGROVE POTTERY AND THE AESTHETICS OF MANUFACTURING

In 1884, the state's recovery from the Civil War, if uneven, was nevertheless evident virtually everywhere and in many different ways.[10] In the years since 1865, the Seagrove potters had created a vast body of work that did more than supply only local needs. Wholesale and retail production, like this jug (photo 20, page 27), had boosted their sales. It is hard to imagine that the potters were not proud of their success.

J. D. Craven ran one such thriving stoneware manufacturing operation. By 1880, the widowed

PHOTO 18: ATTRIBUTED TO JOHN A. CRAVEN, **Fifteen-Gallon Jar with Lid**, *circa 1850. 25⅜ x 13¼ inches (64.5 x 33.7 cm). Stoneware.*
PHOTO © ACKLAND ART MUSEUM, THE UNIVERSITY OF NORTH CAROLINA AT CHAPEL HILL, ACKLAND FUND. 82.31.1

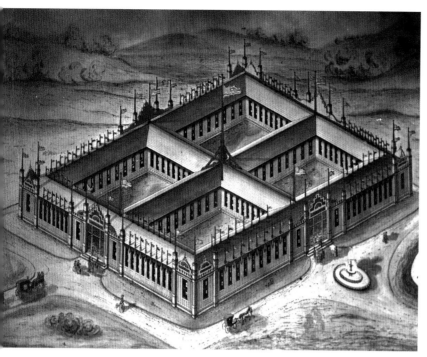

ware was also beautiful, inspiring to touch, and in hindsight amazingly expressive of the potters and their lives. The potters shared the daily experiences of making pottery, backbreaking work that taxed mind, body, and patience. They lived and worked in a place and at a time where life was demanding. Disease was a constant companion, death sometimes brutally sudden for both adults and children. Two of J. D. Craven's brothers died before they were 40. A man might have a bad fall and a broken limb; a stray coal could produce painful burns or burn down a shed like a flash of lightning; influenza, arthritis, or a snake bite could end a productive life. At the same time, the beauty of the place flowed around them: clear water in the creeks, rain from low purple and gray clouds, sheet lightning across the summer night skies. In the spring, white dogwoods brought light into the unfolding, newly green forests; the hot July sun pierced sparkling, steaming trees after a short shower. October's blue skies and leaves burned with nearly the same intensity as a kiln fire. Fog rested in the bottoms and rose from ponds on cool mornings; wild blackberries ripened in the hot sun. Cardinals and bluebirds flashed through trees; natural sounds could be intense, sustained, hypnotic. Life was ruled by chance and possibility. Such an environment, ripe with possibility for variation and exploration, enriched the pottery itself. For each inhabitant, whether a farmer with a successful crop or the woman of the house with a well-made quilt or woven coverlet, the place and the process were physically and emotionally rewarding.

J. D. had remarried. Of his 10 children, two became potters. Other potters at the time, too, were making stoneware as a livelihood. The Browers, Coles, Chriscoes, Foxes, Hayes, Teagues, and Websters continued the profitable economic enterprises they had begun decades earlier. Some potters made more ware than others and some might have been better potters than others, but they were all working. Such popular products as Bull Durham tobacco in small sacks, plaid fabrics from the Holt Mills in Burlington, and the Seagrove stoneware, came of the energy, hope, resilience, and determination that characterized these postwar years.

These characteristics are embodied in the very pottery itself. Piedmont North Carolinians have their own particular speech patterns with flat vowels, nasal inflections, and drawn-out syllables that

Himer Fox, who had lived in Randolph County, married John Craven's widow and they moved to Chatham County. Fox was a wonderful potter whose work, as demonstrated in photo 21, page

THE POTTERS SHARED THE DAILY EXPERIENCES OF MAKING POTTERY, BACKBREAKING WORK THAT TAXED MIND, BODY, AND PATIENCE.

make their speech recognizable. The potters of the Seagrove area evolved their own ceramic language. Most every potter could speak it, but the best pots were memorable: light for their size, well balanced, durable, and strong. Most functional needs could be met by anyone's ware, but the best

28, epitomizes the purposeful simplicity, severity of form, and absence of decoration that resulted from the demands of the production process. And the pot has dignity. The surface of the jar reads like skin that fits tightly, youthfully on the body, a body that rises cleanly from the ground to

PHOTO 20: WILLIAM HENRY CHRISCO, **Two-Gallon Jug**, *circa 1890. 16 x 8 inches (40.6 x 22.9 cm). Salt-glazed stoneware; "2" cogglewheel on side.*
PHOTO BY TIM AYERS, COLLECTION OF NORTH CAROLINA POTTERY CENTER

The ANATOMY OF A VESSEL

*V*essel shapes and parts often have many names, which have been adopted according to the customs of the maker, locale, and era. A few structural terms, though, are very nearly standard in the ceramics lexicon. The ancient form of the vessel has long employed the human body as a convenient metaphor for a pot's parts: collar, lip, rim, neck, shoulder, belly, and foot.

It is possible to develop an even deeper appreciation for a pot by studying how the various parts contribute to its overall success. For instance, a rim might be meekly lipless or flare dramatically into a flowerlike shape. A pot's shoulder can literally hunch around the collar or thrust itself proudly above the belly.

Words that describe decorative techniques usually have more oblique referents, like reeding (lines that circle a neck as if a reed or rope were wound around it) or incising. Handle styles may be either strap, which are open, vertical pieces with end-points attached only at neck and shoulder, or the stronger lug style, in which horizontal "closed" pieces are pressed fully against the body of the vessel, usually in the vicinity of the shoulder.

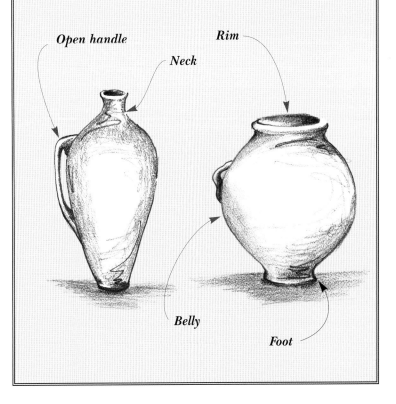

a smoothly flared lip that flows out from the neck. Deep, muscular indentations on the pulled, ridged handles reveal the pressure of the thumbs that pinned them to the body. Its color is that of wet earth, and the band that holds the cracked piece together like a belt emphasizes its balanced shape. This worthy object is like a life, self-reliant and useful.

Two single-handled jugs from the late 19th century also share a puritan simplicity of form. Their strong family resemblance derives from more than their salt-glazed stoneware bodies. The taller one's (photo 22, page 28) minimally shaped handle rises from the shoulder to join the neck, with its down-turned, heavy-lipped spout. Ash drips enrich the cool, brownish gray surface and complement the stony, strong clay that is meant to protect its contents. J. F. Brower's jug (photo 23, page 29), though slightly shorter, has a much more generous spout, and its scant lip is delineated by a lone line. The handle is more open, and a thumbprint firmly joins it to the shoulder of the pot. Among the kiln drips, the potter's stamp becomes a decorative element. Both jugs have the same tactile skin, and their dense clay bodies have sharp profiles that assert their quiet presences. Side by side, their differences help us also see their similarities; they emphasize our awareness that the two makers were unique, creative individuals. Every pot may be like every other pot, but no two pots are alike.

Northeast of Seagrove, in Alamance County, potter Timothy Boggs used the area's lighter clay and it responded differently to his firing and glazing. Boggs' jar is (photo 24) powerful. The clay body's smooth texture reveals an uneven pattern of throwing rings. The splashes of drips, gathered on the neck, spill down the surface, curving slightly as they go, as if drawn by the heat of the fire. Like so much salt-glazed ware, contrasts of dark and light in the skin demand to be touched. In its midst, a large blue droplet—a barely controlled gesture—has the presence of a sudden and

unexpected design. It would be wrong to say that the jar is undecorated. The colors and shapes of the runs and drips make it so pleasant to see, use, and *experience* this jar. As with the memorable Craven vessel on page 24, these pieces have a presence and a beauty drawn from the successful and consistent relationship of form to function—and clay to firing—that satisfies the purpose.

The potters and their families lived with confidence in their understanding of the process and their purpose in making pottery, yet their accomplishments came to be challenged by the very needs that had made their wares profitable. Patterns of life and production that had been in place for a century were slowly succumbing to the need to grow cash crops like cotton, tobacco, and corn, or to raise cattle and hogs. And of course manufacturing changed too. What had been profitable for a few years slowly became unprofitable; one had to be aware of the market and its needs. By 1880, J. D. Craven declared himself not a potter but a farmer. Perhaps the census made a mistake or J. D. was no longer making much pottery or

PHOTO 21: HIMER FOX, **Two-Handled Storage Jar**, *last quarter of 19th century. 12½ x 7 inches (30.5 x 17.8 cm). Salt-glazed stoneware mended with an iron band. Collection of Gallery of Art & Design, North Carolina State University, gift of the Friends of the Gallery Collectors Circle, from the collection of Charles G. Zug III, 2000.042.001*

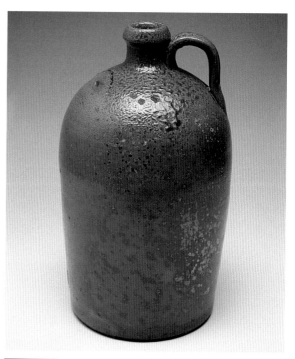

PHOTO 22: UNKNOWN RANDOLPH OR MOORE COUNTY POTTER, **Jug**, *circa 1880. 12¼ x 8 inches (31.1 x 20.3 cm). Salt-glazed stoneware. Collection of Gallery of Art & Design, North Carolina State University, gift of the Friends of the Gallery Collectors Circle, 2004.001.003*

maybe his sons were themselves working busily, but the reassignment seems prophetic. In the Seagrove area, potters were still a few years away from all the changes that industry would bring. They continued work as they had for over a century. They could still put their individual stamps on their wares; manufacturing had not yet taken the work from their hands nor altered the values that had shaped the best of the work into objects of beauty.

NOTES

1. L. McKay Whatley, *The Architectural History of Randolph County North Carolina*, 6

2. Ibid., 8

3. Ibid., 9

4. Ibid.,11

5. Barbara S. Perry, ed. *North Carolina Pottery, The Collection of the Mint Museums*, Chapel Hill, UNC Press, 2004, 194 H1983.190.1172

6. Bishir and Southern, 366.

7. Charles N. Zug, "Traditional Pottery," in Collection of the Mint Museums, 13

8. Charles N. Zug, *Turners and Burners*, 43.

9. Dorothy Auman and Charlie G. Zug, "Nine Generations of Potters: The Cole Family," *Southern Exposure* 5 nos. 2–3 (1977), 166.

10. For example, Moore County alone had 155 miles of railroad by 1898 and eight different railroads served the area.

PHOTO 23: J. F. BROWER, **Jug**, *second half of 19th century. Height, 11 inches (27.9 cm). Salt-glazed stoneware; "J. F. Brower" stamp with a "1" stamped on shoulder. Collection of Gallery of Art & Design, North Carolina State University, gift of Ray Wilkinson, 2001.001.007*

PHOTO 24: ATTRIBUTED TO TIMOTHY BOGGS, **Preserve Jar**, *circa 1840–1870. 10¼ x 6 inches (26 x 15.2 cm). Salt-glazed stoneware. Collection of Gallery of Art & Design, North Carolina State University, gift of the Friends of the Gallery Collectors Circle, 2005.012.003*

CHAPTER 2

A NEW CENTURY
IN SEAGROVE

PHOTO 1: **Farm Security Administration Rural Arts Exhibition at U.S. Department of Agriculture, 1937.**
COURTESY LIBRARY OF CONGRESS, LC-USW316-056309-B

In 1900, Seagrove was still a little crossroads in a region of modest farms. Every day the train that made its way through the countryside on its way from Asheboro to Robbins brought new stimulus to this long-isolated spot. Improvements in transportation spurred the growth of a new market for ceramics, as new materials became available to the potters, and their finished work could be more easily shipped to other markets. More newspapers, magazines, farm journals, and other publications appeared as new resources for ideas and information, along with exhibitions of rural arts that included North Carolina work (photo 1). The area was still home to working potters from such families as the Craven, Cole, Owens, Chrisco, and Teague.

Between 1900 and 1950, Seagrove potters watched their fortunes rise and fall as they survived Prohibition and the Great Depression. They sent their sons to work in furniture factories, textile mills, and tobacco plants, and to fight in World Wars I and II. Entrepreneurial potters opened their shops to new ideas and methods as they slowly but relentlessly moved in new directions. Success might come, but failure was just as possible.

Social and economic change continued but slowly in the three-county area around Seagrove. Randolph County's textile mills in Asheboro and Franklinton prospered. Although a few automobiles were in use, the Tyson and Jones Buggy Company in Carthage, the Moore County seat, remained a busy enterprise. In Montgomery County, the Norfolk Southern Railway finally connected this picturesque area in the Uwharries to Charlotte and Raleigh so that the county's young lumber businesses could thrive. In the early 1920s, the county seats of Moore and Montgomery built new courthouses (photo 2), each a tribute to the enterprise and optimism that flowed from the growing economy. Farther afield, other great economic drivers were flourishing: textiles in Siler City, Burlington, Charlotte, Gastonia, and Greensboro; furniture in Thomasville, Lexington, and High Point; tobacco in Winston-Salem and Durham. Seagrove itself was at the center of the region's wood-products network, which harvested the pine forests that surrounded farms and framed roads. Sections of new railroad sprouted like weeds all over the state, using the wooden crossties the town was known for.

PHOTO 2: **Benton and Benton Architects, Troy, Montgomery County Courthouse, 1921.**
COURTESY OF THE NORTH CAROLINA STATE ARCHIVES, N.78.12.1267

PHOTO 3: DOROTHEA LANGE,
Pottery Butter Churn on Porch of Negro Tenant Family, *1939.*
COURTESY LIBRARY OF CONGRESS, LC-USF34-020142-E

PHOTO 4:
Photographer unknown, Grove Park Inn and Asheville Golf Course, circa 1915.
COURTESY OF THE GROVE PARK INN RESORT & SPA

PHOTO 5: **Carolina Hotel (with subsequent additions), 1899–1900. Kendall, Taylor & Stevens, Boston.**

PHOTO COURTESY OF TUFTS ARCHIVES OF THE GIVEN MEMORIAL LIBRARY

Farming's continuing difficulties, on the other hand, worsened with the Great Depression. Since the 1880s, an increasing number of farmers were growing cotton or tobacco, which could be sold for cash rather than the kinds of food-and-feed crops that had been needed to sustain the family. As self-sufficiency declined, tenancy increased (photo 3, page 31). Dependent on wholesale and retail markets, the farmer became a part of an economic system and regional and national trends he had no influence over. Many farmers turned to making whiskey from the corn they grew. From the moment that industrialization became a desideratum for the Seagrove region, traditional markets that had once supported a potter and his family (or had provided a major source of extra income) were threatened. Manufacturing stimulated the development of a society of consumers who preferred manufactured tin, glass, and "china" wares. These store-bought items represented a new way of life and seemed more attractive, more durable, and more progressive than the traditional functional earthenware and stoneware that filled the kitchens and storage sheds of families who still lived rural lives.

As towns grew and mill villages gathered around the textile and furniture factories, the villagers created new community centers, such as churches, to counter the tensions, anxieties, and hostilities that emerged from living in towns and working in the demanding, noisy, dirty, dangerous mills. These natural community centers supported the increasing influence of the women's temperance movement. In North Carolina, the movement succeeded in waves, first eliminating the sale of liquor (except in incorporated towns) in 1903, then abolishing it in communities under 1,000 (making 68 of the state's 98 counties dry), and finally securing statewide prohibition in 1909. Passage of the 18th Amendment in 1919 finally decimated one of the potters' major, although already declining, markets. The Busbees, who founded the Jugtown Pottery about 1922, estimated that 50 potters were put out of business by Prohibition. But just as the end of whiskey jug production seemed to doom some potters' livelihoods, the growth of tourism changed the chemistry in the region.

THE ADVENT OF TOURISM

In the southeastern portion of Moore County, a layer of deep sandy soil left by the retreating ancient ocean had formed the Sandhills, an area with a microclimate of warm, mild winters. In the last quarter of the 19th century, the railroad made it easier to harvest its abundant pine forests. John T. Patrick, a developer from Wadesboro, North Carolina, bought land and planned a town he called Southern Pines as a retreat for recuperating consumptives. It was an enterprising venture similar to those of the hotel builders and boarding-house keepers who had capitalized on the clean air of the beautiful mountains around Asheville, another early tourist mecca, located in the western part of the state (photo 4).

Southern Pines grew slowly, but was soon joined by Pinehurst, "A New England Village in the South" designed by the firm of the renowned landscape architect Frederick Law Olmsted, who had recently planned the landscape at George Vanderbilt's Biltmore House (and accompanying farm and village) in Asheville. Olmsted's firm turned the Moore County pine lands into a verdant wintertime retreat for golfers, horseback riders, and wealthy health-seekers from the Northeast (photo 5).

Such seasonal visitors brought tastes and ideas influenced by the Colonial Revival and the Arts and Crafts movements, which reinforced the value of craftsmanship and handmade work that predated the Industrial Revolution.[1] They built Arts and Crafts–inspired bungalows and wood-framed or red-brick Colonial Revival cottages (photo 6). The visitors enjoyed a busy social season of hunts and golf and shooting matches. They also visited the potters whose work represented the survival of a long tradition that they found quaint, important, and attractive. Many of these people valued America's Anglo-Saxon roots and its pre-Revolutionary architecture, metalwork, ceramics, textiles, and furniture. Thirty-five rough miles to the homes of many potters did not deter visitors from Southern Pines and Pinehurst, who brought ideas for new pots with them.

Tourism also stimulated better marketing. Articles appeared in magazines about North Carolina pottery, and sometimes catalogs and roadside stands were used for display and sales. It was during this period that economic imperatives

PHOTO 6: **Pinehurst streetscape, no date.**
PHOTO COURTESY OF TUFTS ARCHIVES OF THE GIVEN MEMORIAL LIBRARY

PHOTO 7: **Pottery display from an advertising brochure, created after 1926, showing the sales room of the North State Pottery Company, Sanford, North Carolina.** COURTESY OF THE NORTH CAROLINA STATE ARCHIVES, N.73.8.1184

 NORTH STATE, LIKE SEVERAL OTHER FORWARD-LOOKING PRACTITIONERS, DECLARED THAT THEIRS WAS AN OLD INDUSTRY IN THE PROCESS OF RENEWING ITSELF

PHOTO 8: **Henry Cooper and the cabin facade at Philadelphia's 1926 Sesqui-Centennial International Exposition.**

COURTESY OF THE NORTH CAROLINA STATE ARCHIVES, N.75.9.338

plus rising academic and aesthetic interest in the historicity of American craft were beginning to stimulate practical solutions to the threat of mass-produced ware. In October 1925, the newly founded North State Pottery in Sanford exhibited at the North Carolina State Fair (photo 7), which was the successor to the Exposition of 1884. During the fair, they sold between 1,000 and 2,000 pieces: floor and table vases, jars, and pitchers. North State, like several other forward-looking practitioners, now declared that theirs was an old industry in the process of renewing itself (photo 8).

New Forms for a New Market

Prohibition and the increased availability of manufactured goods caused the potters to wonder, What would sell? Barry Huffman, who wrote about the potters of the Catawba Valley during this same period, summed up the problem—and the solution—in a single word: scale. Cream risers and churns don't travel well, but miniature twig furniture and ceramic jugs and mugs make great souvenirs (photo 9). The question, however, was more than simply one of size. The new clientele influenced which colors, textures, and decorations were used too. By the beginning of the Great Depression, many of the types of pots prevalent before 1900 were either no longer in the potters' repertoires or so changed as to be unrecognizable. This was, of course, the potters' great strength: their long-established tradition provided rich resources for new forms. But the potters had no illusions; only those who were able to recognize and adapt to changes in style (and had the technical means to do so) could ultimately triumph.

Three Seagrove enterprises, the potteries of C. R. Auman, J. B. Cole, and Jugtown, chose three different (but related) strategies for making what was then called "art pottery," a term that first came into use in the late 19th century. It was associated with the Arts and Crafts Movement and with a revival of handmade pottery that was beautiful, decorative, and collectible. Some of the first pieces were the decorated wares made by potteries like the Rookwood Company in Ohio, the Grueby Pottery in Massachusetts, and the pottery at Newcombe College in Louisiana (photo 10). In the United States, art pottery belonged with the furniture of Stickley or Limberts, and with Tiffany Studio glass. It was found in homes designed by Greene and Greene of California and Frank Lloyd Wright in Illinois. Artisans in textiles and metal also espoused similar ideals and rejected mass-produced wares.

The work of the three Seagrove potteries reflected the influence of art pottery's forms and colors. Tourism alone was probably not the only source for their awareness, since magazines and newspapers contained images associated with the style. These potteries seem to have also been influenced by the design ideas of the

PHOTO 9: ATTRIBUTED TO WELCH POTTERY, **Miniature Whiskey Jug,** *1901. Height, 2½ inches (6.4 cm). Salt-glazed stoneware; inscribed "Buy this for me, Pa, 1901". © North Carolina Museum of History*

PHOTO 10: GRUEBY POTTERY, **Vase**, *circa 1920. 10½ x 7½ inches (26.7 x 19 cm). Stoneware; elephant skin glaze; stamped "Grueby". Collection of Gallery of Art & Design, North Carolina State University, gift of the Friends of the Gallery Collectors Circle, 1995.009.003*

PHOTO 11: **J. B. Cole unloading a groundhog kiln, circa 1920s.**
NORTH CAROLINA COLLECTION, PACK MEMORIAL PUBLIC LIBRARY, ASHEVILLE, NORTH CAROLINA

Colonial Revival, a period marked by reverence for surviving artifacts of pre–Revolutionary War days, including log cabins, rustic "colonial" saltbox houses, and early-American redware, furniture, and silver. Housewares were collected and placed in revival settings in a kind of seriously self-conscious, Eurocentric (and especially Anglophile) awareness of America's cultural roots. The New England Village of Pinehurst epitomized this attitude. Nevertheless, cultural reinventions and the currents of thought represented by both the Arts and Crafts Movement and the Colonial Revival—both of which lost energy after the first World War—formed part of the background for a new kind of pottery making.

C. R. AUMAN POTTERY

C. R. Auman, descended from a local potting family, was an entrepreneur. With money he had made in other businesses, Auman decided to establish a pottery near Seagrove and the Michfield (sometimes spelled Mitchfield) clay deposit.[2] He hired Frank Richardson and Pascal Marable, two skilled and expert local potters, to set up the business. It may have been Marable, a potter active for at least two decades, who suggested to Auman that he buy the land that held a deep vein of clean, very light-colored, stoneware clay. Two kilns were constructed: an unusual double-walled bottle kiln and the more typical groundhog kiln like this one at J. B. Cole's (photo 11). Although the round kiln looked as if it had been lifted right out of England's long-established ceramics industry, the structure seemed at home in the Piedmont. Still, the design was an anomaly.

Auman's sons, Ray and James, and Lorenzo (Wren) Cole (of the potting Cole family), were hired to throw and fire. Sometime in the late 1920s, Floyd Hilton, from the Catawba Valley, joined the enterprise. These men made clear lead–glazed small jars, pie plates, mugs, and ovoid vases from buff earthenware clay. They also created traditional functional stoneware during this period. Finished pieces were stamped, on the bottom or side, with the Auman name inside an oval.

Between 1920 and 1927, the Auman pottery also made clean-looking, ash-free art pottery from buff-colored stoneware. If salt glazed, the smooth, matte surfaces on the clay were sometimes warmly colored peach or pink. Another type was lead-glazed buff or shiny yellow ware (photo 12) dotted or striped with either cobalt or manganese glazes. The shapes—whether vases, candlesticks, sugar bowls, or creamers—were just as decorative as they were useful. A bottle kiln was likely to have fired the art pottery, since such a saggar-style kiln prevents fly ash (from burning wood) from set-

PHOTO 12: AUMAN POTTERY, **Fluted Vase**, *circa 1925. 6 x 5¾ inches (15.2 x 14.6 cm). Stoneware; clear lead glaze with cobalt decoration. Collection of Gallery of Art & Design, North Carolina State University, gift of the Friends of the Gallery Collectors Circle, 2002.002.004*

 CREAM RISERS AND CHURNS DON'T TRAVEL WELL, BUT MINIATURE TWIG FURNITURE AND CERAMIC JUGS AND MUGS MAKE GREAT SOUVENIRS.

tling on ware. The bottle kiln may have been only partly successful because some of the pots show evidence of fly ash, but a groundhog could not have produced consistently clean surfaces.

Auman's success depended on the skill and adaptability of the young potters who worked for him. These men were accustomed to throwing traditional ware like jugs and churns, which could easily be transformed into tall, tapered vases. A greater challenge was the wide, flattened lip that needed to replace the churn's neck. To keep clay forms with thinner elements from warping during the firing process, the intense heat must be built up slowly, sustained consistently, and cooled just as carefully. The vases shown in photo 13, with their wide, flattened rims or lips, are strictly decorative, useful only to hold flowers or to stand on a shelf. Their feet, too, are less broad and the bellies taper down more sharply than traditional wares, which usually have bases as broad as their shoulders.

PHOTO 13: AUMAN POTTERY, **Two Vases**, *circa 1925. Left: 8½ x 6 inches (21.6 x 15.2 cm) in diameter; right: 6½ x 6 inches (16.5 x 15.2 cm) in diameter. Stoneware; clear lead glaze with cobalt decoration. Collection of Cynthia and Thomas Edwards*

PHOTO 16: AUMAN POTTERY, **Basket**, *circa 1927. 3½ x 6 inches (8.9 x 15.2 cm). Earthenware; clear lead glaze with applied color. Collection of Gallery of Art & Design, North Carolina State University, gift of the Friends of the Gallery Collectors Circle, 2001.0038.001*

PHOTO 14: AUMAN POTTERY, *circa 1925. Left:* **Cup and Saucer**. **Cup,** *3½ x 4½ inches (8.9 x 11.4 cm). Right:* **Mug**, *3 ½ x 4 inches (8.9 x 10.2 cm). Both: stoneware; clear lead glaze with cobalt wash. Collection of Cynthia and Thomas Edwards*

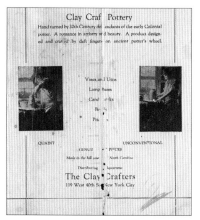

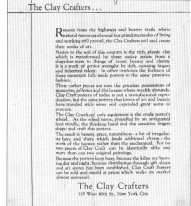

PHOTO 15: **Clay Crafters advertisement, circa late 1920s, featuring C. R. Auman lead-glaze pottery.**
COURTESY OF SOUTHERN FOLK POTTERY COLLECTOR SOCIETY, SOCIETY RESEARCH FILES

Modest-size art pieces, 12 to 18 inches tall, became standard. Ovoid and globular vases rested on small round feet. Auman's potters made simple bottles and small cups without handles, or high-shouldered vases, flattened at the top, with rimless openings. Some vases had attached handles, almost like those used on pitchers, but no form appears to be a direct derivation of any particular older Seagrove-area form, which suggests that the potters were trying new shapes by looking at magazines and making variations on traditional shapes.

Auman's men also continued to make tableware (photo 14). It is well-balanced pottery, unusually light for its size, and fairly thin walled. The almost perfectly smooth exterior surfaces resemble mass-produced, slip-cast ceramic wares, just as their trailed drips and stripes recall the sprigs and flowers of inexpensive "china."

Auman Pottery's wares were sold not only in Seagrove but also at Clay Crafters, a retail outlet for pottery in New York City. Their 1920s-era advertisement (photo 15) offered unique, hand-crafted wares by potters working in a centuries-old tradition. Its images and text were drawn from symbols of American heritage ("Hand turned by 20th Century descendants of the early Colonial potter") and associated pottery with both an Anglo-Saxon heritage and a crafts revival that was by then quite popular in the Southern Appalachians.[3]

Then, perhaps as early as 1926 or 1927, an unusually decorated type of ware became part of the Auman Pottery's repertoire. "A chemist came to work at Charlie Auman's shop for months, and they were doing some pretty things from his work. He made a marbelized [sic] glaze—white, brown, and blue. It sort of swerved around. Must have been a clay slip with some lead because it was glossy. They fired it with the regular salt glaze, but he would not share in that with anyone. He went in and boarded up the windows so they couldn't see what he was putting together. He'd lock the door when he went in and lock it when he come out."[4]

The little basket in photo 16 might be an experimental piece in earthenware, because its colored surface decoration is so much bolder than earlier Auman work. The form itself, similar to that of a glass candy or flower basket, abounds in variations typical of the work of potters in the Seagrove area. Its heavily mottled surface decoration suggests that sometime in the mid-1920s Auman had met Charles B. Masten, the secretive chemist from the Midwest.[5]

Masten (photo 17) had married a local woman, and their summer visits to the Seagrove area signaled the beginning of a brief but significant period of collaboration at C. R. Auman's pottery—one that produced a totally new type of ware. Auman's young potters found in Masten a keen collaborator. Their supply of Michfield clay was an excellent stoneware clay, and Masten had mastered his craft sufficiently to be able to formulate slips and glazes that were chemically compatible with it.

For a few summers, Masten decorated pots that had been prepared for him by Auman employees. Those skilled potters produced simple and elegant shapes, globular or ovoid and devoid of complex lips, spouts, or handles (photo 18). It was as if the collaborators had agreed that these simple shapes would provide the best kind of field for the beauty and complexity of their intense glazes. The secrecy surrounding both Masten the man and his glazing process was unusual in a community where practical knowledge was usually a shared commodity. Few pieces from this collaboration survive and little is known about their production. The work was unlike any other made in Seagrove at that time. Clearly, it was art pottery, beautiful and collectible.

PHOTO 17: **Charles B. and Ida Masten in a photo probably made on the occasion of their wedding in June, 1895.** COURTESY OF CLARICE REDDING

CLEARLY, IT WAS ART POTTERY, BEAUTIFUL AND COLLECTIBLE.

PHOTO 18: AUMAN POTTERY-MASTEN COLLABORATION, **Vase**, *circa 1928. 4¾ x 4 (12 x 10.2 cm). Cobalt- and salt-glazed stoneware. Collection of Gallery of Art & Design, North Carolina State University, gift of the Friends of the Gallery Collectors Circle, 1998.023.001*

PHOTO 19: AUMAN POTTERY-MASTEN COLLABORA-
TION, **Ovoid Vase**, *circa 1928–1930. 14 x 8 inches
(35.6 x 20.3 cm). Cobalt- and salt-glazed stoneware.
Collection of Gallery of Art & Design, North
Carolina State University, gift of the grandchildren
of Lillie Graham and Claude Auman,
2001.020.001*

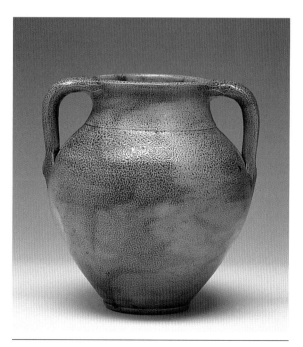

PHOTO 20: AUMAN POTTERY-MASTEN
COLLABORATION, **Vase with Attached Handles**,
*circa 1928. 7 x 7 inches (17.8 x 17.8 cm).
Salt-glazed stoneware with cobalt swirl. Collection
of Gallery of Art & Design, North Carolina State
University, gift of the Friends of the Gallery
Collectors Circle, 1999.022.001*

The Auman-Masten pieces have one of four types
of decoration: solid, swirled, swirled with drips,
and drips over solid colors. The solid sheath of
glaze color might be intense and sometimes a very
shiny blue (from cobalt; photo 19), mauve (manganese), green (copper), or the plain pale gray of a
salt-only glaze. All the solid-colored wares also
have the characteristic "orange-peel" surface of
salt-glazed, wood-fired stoneware—a direct echo of
the 19th century. They are intensely sculptural
and tactile. The strong color is never perfectly
even and the surface seems almost oily, as if the
color could be moved around on the surface of an
otherwise intractable form that is solidly resistant
to change. However, this work usually has a continuity and unity of surface, form, and material that
appears similar to Rookwood-style art pottery,
although Rookwood employed a slip-cast mold
production method and hand-applied decoration.

THE WORK THAT SURVIVES SUGGESTS THERE WAS A TENDENCY TO CONCENTRATE ON ART WARE

A two-handled vase (photo 20), with its pale
ground and muted, mostly one-color glaze, recalls
marbleized (sometimes called "swirl") ware,
though neither of these decorative techniques was
common in the Seagrove area. The variegated
effect was created when one or more colors of
water-based glaze or slip were floated on an oily
bath and the unglazed pot, rotated on the surface,
picked up an uneven decorative pattern that
resulted from the separation created by the oil and
water. True swirlware, popular in early 20th-centu-
ry work from North Carolina's Catawba Valley, was
made in a different way, with two different colors
of clay only partly blended together. Usually,
Auman's swirlware was made of stoneware, though
there were also earthenware pieces on which veils
of cobalt were mixed with copper or other colors
to obtain a more variegated surface. Such vases are
relatives of Chinese blue-and-white ware with

hand-applied cobalt decoration. The color moves around the vase's surface, heavier here and thinner there, almost syrupy or drippy in some places and nearly transparent in others.

The vases with controlled drips are riveting. The balanced consistency of the runs as they fall from a thick collar and divide the surface emphasizes its volume (photo 21). More than any other Auman type, this work is strongly tactile. When the drips are combined with swirl decoration, they suggest landscapes, similar in effect to a Rookwood Pottery Scenic Vellum vase (photo 22), or a piece from the Moss and Moon series produced by the Newcombe Pottery. Masten, however, created a different kind of landscape, although it is still oriental in feeling. The complex swirls disappear and reappear behind the screen created by the drips. The shape's simplicity reinforces the elegance of the surface, with wonderful contrasts of smoother, slicker, watery cobalt decoration beneath the drips. The form is precise and clean; the effect of the changing surface organic and living.

The Auman shop was making art pottery before Masten joined it, but his intervention elevated the work. The pottery's lifeblood had been a combination of useful ware and art pottery, but the work that survives suggests that there was a tendency to concentrate on art ware that had no local precedent. With the coming of the Great Depression, Auman quickly went broke. Within a few years he sold the site of his pottery, along with the clay bed, to the Pomona Terra-Cotta Company.[6]

THE BUSBEES AND JUGTOWN POTTERY

Juliana, born Julia Adeline Royster, and Jacques, born James Littlejohn Busbee, were from prominent Raleigh families. Jacques was educated as a painter at the National Academy of Design, the Art Students League, and the Chase School in New York City. Juliana attended St. Mary's Junior College, a private school for girls, and studied photography with an uncle. They were married in 1910 and set about to establish themselves in the world.

As Jacques painted and traveled around North Carolina, he lectured on art and collected old North Carolina pottery. To revive interest in the

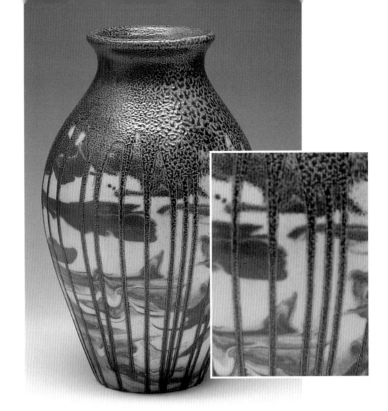

PHOTO 21: AUMAN POTTERY-MASTEN COLLABORATION, **Vase**, *circa 1928–1930. 11½ x 7 inches (29.2 x 17.8 cm). Salt-glazed stoneware with controlled manganese drip over cobalt decoration. Loaned by Annie Hagar Blunk*

PHOTO 22: ROOKWOOD POTTERY, **Scenic Vellum Vase**, *1921. Height, 9¾ inches (24.8 cm). Porcelain; painted by Sallie Coyne; stamped "xxi 829 v". Collection of Gallery of Art & Design, North Carolina State University, gift of the Friends of the Gallery Collectors Circle, 1991.009.001*

PHOTO 24: **Jessie Tarbox Beals, Alice Sit by the Fire: The Village Store in Greenwich Village, circa 1916–1920.**
© MUSEUM OF THE CITY OF NEW YORK. MUSEUM PURCHASE WITH FUNDS DONATED BY LISA AND ERIC GREEN 95.127.3

PHOTO 23: UNKNOWN JUGTOWN POTTER, **Pie Plate**, *1930.*
10¼ inches (26 cm) in diameter. Earthenware; lead glaze;
stamped "Jugtown". Collection of Gallery of Art & Design,
North Carolina State University, transfer from the North
Carolina Museum of Art, 1984.009.067

folk crafts of the state, Juliana traveled a bit as Chairman of the Art Department of the Federation of Women's Clubs. In 1915, while acting as a juror for the Davidson County Fair in Lexington, Juliana found brilliant orange-glazed pie plates at the local hardware store. She bought all of them for 10 cents each. Pieces like this pie plate (photo 23), which were produced later at Jugtown, fired her imagination and changed the Busbees' lives.[7]

Juliana's earthenware pie plate was merely a typical product of the region's ceramic cottage industry, yet when Juliana returned to Raleigh with it, the Busbees found their future: the couple committed themselves with "passionate patriotism" to saving North Carolina's dying craft of pottery making. Finding little interest or support among their North Carolina friends and acquaintances, they moved to New York in 1916. There, they became dealers in Seagrove-area earthenware, which they sold in the Village Store, Juliana's tea shop in Greenwich Village. The shop was successful, and they soon moved uptown, to East 60th Street (photo 24).

Jacques first visited Seagrove in May 1917; according to his account, he was first suspected of spying for the Germans, but he was soon able to convince the local people that he only wanted to find pottery to sell. In the New York shop, Juliana marketed these wares with great acumen. The shop's interior was an evocation of the Colonial Revival for architecture and interior design in vogue at the time. Juliana told customers that the earthenware was made by Seagrove potters, descended from British potters who had brought the craft from their homeland, and who had practiced it since the Revolutionary War.[8]

Both Busbees were sympathetic to and conversant with the philosophy of the American Arts and Crafts Movement. Like its English cousin, this reformist movement promoted the unique, the handmade, and the artful as means to a wholesome life.[9] Juliana wrote, "What greater compliment can be bestowed than to say of a person, He or she has a 'genius for life,'—that the surroundings and the individual are in harmony." The Busbees aimed toward this life. The vernacular ware they found in Seagrove must have seemed like a message from the venerable past.

The flow of wares to New York from the Seagrove area was, however, unpredictable and fraught with difficulty. After a few years of struggling to maintain both the shop in the city and their contacts with their suppliers (particularly the potter J. H. Owen), the Busbees decided to move to Seagrove. They reported that the pottery tradition there was "moribund," even though both the Auman and Cole potteries were active when they arrived and other potters, too, were still practicing the craft.

In 1921 or '22 in Moore County, near the Randolph County line and the Old Plank Road, Jacques and Juliana leased land from the Scott family. They built a pottery shop with a dirt floor, two kick wheels, board shelves, and a cast-iron stove. This simple establishment became the birthplace of Jugtown Pottery.[10] In 1924, they bought some seven acres from the Scotts, who also built a log house for the couple (photo 25). Then they set about to solve the same problems that C. R. Auman and J. B. Cole faced: getting pottery made and sold. The biggest questions were: What would be made and how would it look?

PHOTO 25: **The Busbee House, Jugtown, from a post card dated 1938 and postmarked Steeds, North Carolina, written by Juliana Busbee to Mrs. W. K. Rivers, Atlanta.** ARCHIVES, GALLERY OF ART & DESIGN, NORTH CAROLINA STATE UNIVERSITY

PHOTO 26: **Oscar L. Bachelder, Interior View of Omar Khayyam Pottery, Candler, North Carolina, 1927.** COLLECTION OF GEORGE AND DEBBIE VIALL

PHOTO 27: **Oscar L. Bachelder, Exterior View of Omar Khayyam Pottery, Candler, North Carolina, 1927.** COLLECTION OF GEORGE AND DEBBIE VIALL

And *who* would make it? J. H. Owen, who had supplied wares from his own pottery to Juliana's New York Village Shop, died just as the Busbees were setting up. They hired Charlie Teague and Benjamin W. Owen (J. H. Owen's nephew), whose families had been in the area since the early 19th century. Ben and Charlie worked together at the pottery for a few years, but by the late 1920s, it was Ben who had became the Busbees' close collaborator. Matching the skills that produced traditional ware with the Busbees' desire to create new forms was a challenging undertaking. Potters at C. R. Auman's and at J. B. Cole's potteries faced a comparable situation.

Juliana and Jacques looked to many sources for new forms and colors. Almost a decade earlier, Juliana had visited Oscar L. Bachelder at his pottery in Candler, near Asheville (photos 26 and 27, page 43). Bachelder, inspired by the Arts and Crafts Movement, had abandoned production work to make art pottery. He participated in the Boston Arts and Crafts show and exhibited in Chicago, where he won a prize at the Art Institute. The financially successful Bachelder also mentored several potters. A bust of Omar Khayyam adorned the Candler shed, given to him by sculptor Augustus Saint Gaudens' brother, who came to study with him.

Bachelder experimented with forms and glazes, making vases with simple shapes, candle stands, lidded pots, and a variety of smaller objects. To get the glaze colors and surface transformations he wanted, Bachelder frequently double- and triple-dipped his pots in Albany slip (photo 28). Juliana, inspired by the simplicity of his forms and the vigor with which he proclaimed his goal, collected examples and pictures of Bachelder's work.

Another pottery tradition that sparked the Busbees' imagination was the highly regarded Asian pottery. It certainly offered many possibilities. Jacques turned to the ceramics of early dynasties—Han, T'ang, Sung—whose wares are characterized by simple, strong forms, monochromatic coloring, and an absence of decoration (photo 29). Busbee perceived a direct connection between these forms and the simple, powerful stoneware found around Seagrove. He believed that Chinese and Korean wares could inform the potters and enable them to reshape the pervasive Seagrove traditions.[11]

The Busbees' vision emerged slowly, by trial and error. If the results are any indication, their reactions to the "oriental translations" (as they came to be called) must have been of great excitement, ones tempered by thoughtful and positive suggestions. Just as C. R. Auman's potters had thrown ware that became alchemical when paired with Charlie Masten's glazes, Ben Owen's collaboration with the Busbees was magical, explosive, profound, and powerful. Owen was the master potter (photo 30), interpreting, exploring, and expanding the Busbee vision—one that was for the most part profitable enough to enable Jugtown to weather the Great Depression and World War II.

From the beginning, the Jugtown inventory relied on familiar traditional earthenware and stoneware forms, such as pie and "bent" plates (photo 31), small whiskey jugs, jars, platters, pitchers and

PHOTO 31: JUGTOWN POTTERY, **Bent Plate**, *circa 1950s. 10½ x 8½ x 1½ inches (26.7 x 21.6 x 3.8 cm). Earthenware; clear glaze; stamped "Jugtown". Collection of Gallery of Art & Design, North Carolina State University, gift of Banks and Louise Talley, 2003.006.004*

PHOTO 32: JUGTOWN POTTERY, *circa 1930s. Left: Cup and Saucer. Cup, 2½ x 3½ inches (6.4 x 8.9 cm) diameter; saucer, 6 inches (15.2 cm) in diameter. Earthenware; tobacco spit glaze; stamped "Jugtown". Center: Lidded Bowl, 2½ x 6 inches (6.4 x 15.2 cm) diameter. Earthenware; orange glaze; stamped "Jugtown". Right: Mug, 3½ x 3½ inches (8.9 x 8.9 cm). Earthenware; tobacco spit glaze. All collection of Gallery of Art & Design, North Carolina State University, (left to right) 1984.9.42A&B; 1984.9.16 A&B; transfer from the North Carolina Museum of Art, gift of the Friends of the Gallery Collectors Circle, 2000.004.004*

THE KEY TO JUGTOWN'S SUCCESS WAS BEN OWEN'S INFORMED INTERPRETATIONS OF ASIAN WARE USING TRADITIONAL SEAGROVE FORMS

other kinds of tableware, as well as larger crocks and churns. Although a lucrative market for whiskey jugs had been halted by the Prohibition, the Busbees realized that if other potters were surviving by making a variety of work, then they could too. Thus they set about with Ben Owen to develop Jugtown's line of functional tableware with several glazes, and added new forms like footed berry bowls, lidded bowls adapted from Asian-style rice bowls, cookie jars, sugar bowls, and creamers. The popular glazes were "tobacco spit," a bright brownish orange (photo 32, page 45); buff yellow; frogskin (a greenish-brown-

speckled color obtained from salted Albany slip, which was an "imported" clay shipped from a site in New York state); mirror black; orange; the dense, creamy Chinese white; and gray stoneware, which was sometimes called Craven ware.

Functional ware provided a supportive backbone, both literally and figuratively, for the Busbees' aesthetic aspirations. Constantly throwing and firing so many different shapes, Ben Owen honed his skills and trained his eye to be able to adapt images from magazines and objects from museums.

The Busbees' very first potter/supplier, J. H. Owen, had made work that suggested possibilities beyond useful ware, and what he made is a sort of documentation of the struggle to achieve new and successful forms. For example, this floor vase (photo 33)—sporting four handles decorated with cobalt splashes, a slightly flared neck, and a base too narrow to be very practical as a storage vessel—is very near to being a churn. Compared with a new variation on the same form, the proportions of the vase are more robust (photo 34), and its neck flares even wider. Applied bands, looking as if they were made by pressing clay coils between thumb and finger, circle the shoulder. This pot might be a storage jar, but the added decorative elements make it something more, and that "something more" is the essence of what the Busbees and Ben Owen were searching for.

By taking him to New York's museums and the Freer Gallery in Washington, D.C., and looking at books on the subject, Jacques and Juliana introduced Ben Owen to 16th- and 17th-century Chinese, Korean, and even earlier ceramic traditions. Ben made drawings and photographs of the forms that he studied, then used them to make bowls, vases, urns, and wine jars. Such Asian forms resembled Seagrove's traditional shapes and were well suited to the area's clay and firing techniques, but the new forms also inspired Jugtown's useful ware. There is a sense of flow, back and forth, between potter, tradition, the form, and its source.

PHOTO 33: ATTRIBUTED TO J. H. OWEN, **Four-Handled Floor Vase**, *circa 1920. Height, 18 inches (45.7 cm). Lead-glazed earthenware; cobalt decoration on handles. Collection of Cynthia and Thomas Edwards*

Jugtown tableware was usually made in earthenware and the art pottery in the more durable stoneware. Jacques worked on glazes, seeking to find the right colors for each form, while Juliana developed some decorations and continued in her role as "marketing" expert. But the key to Jugtown's success was Ben Owen's informed interpretations of Asian ware using traditional Seagrove forms.

Making a well-thrown, glazed, and fired form that served its intended purpose required experience, tenacity, and the ability to learn from mistakes, and these characteristics served the traditional potter very well. This process of adaptation and integration was complex yet improvisational, and the aesthetically pleasing and unselfconscious stoneware of J. D. Craven and Himer Fox also modeled possibilities that Ben Owen could draw on.

The pair of J. H. Owen floor vases illuminate the problem Ben Owen faced when he sought to create a more artistic, decorative form. The height and dignity of J. H.'s vase (photo 34) is marred by the awkward placement of the handles, the relation of the neck to body and shoulder, and the applied ropelike decoration. This form came to be called a "Persian Jar," in reference to the then-common practice of considering Persia as part of the Orient.

Comparing J. H.'s vase to one made by Ben Owen (photo 35) shows how Ben modified the form. Both are tall with small bases; they proclaim that they are neither churns nor storage crocks. The applied decoration around the shoulder of the orange pot sits there uneasily, but the one on the blue pot defines its shoulder and is supported by the belly's swelling. The biggest difference between them, of course, is in the neck, which Ben elongated. It rises fluidly to a modest rolled lip that just caps the

PHOTO 34: ATTRIBUTED TO J. H. OWEN, **Four-Handled Floor Vase**, *circa 1920. 16 x 11 inches (40.6 x 27.9 cm). Lead-glazed earthenware. Collection of Gallery of Art & Design, North Carolina State University, gift of Ray Wilkinson, 2001.001.001*

PHOTO 35: ATTRIBUTED TO BEN OWEN OF JUGTOWN POTTERY, **Persian Jar**, *circa 1930s. 16 x 12 inches (40.6 x 30.5 cm). Chinese blue–glazed stoneware; stamped "Jugtown". Collection of Gallery of Art & Design, North Carolina State University, transfer from the North Carolina Museum of Art, 1998.001.083*

energy of the continuous upward swell from base to belly to neck. Its scale alone is an impressive accomplishment. The mottled red/green/blue glaze that Jacques called Chinese blue envelopes the form, stopping short of the pot's base, letting it show as if to emphasize its clay origin, to contrast with the glaze, and to emulate its source. The glaze is like a hard stone-jade or marble—this jar is plainly more precious than earthenware or plain salt-glazed stoneware could ever be.

Even small changes altered a jar's appearance. The joints of handles once broad enough to carry the weight of a full jar (photo 36), became more delicate, the base tapered slightly more, proclaiming that the function was not service but beauty. Decorative elements were more confident, crisp, symmetrical. Even the variations in color between the two affected their appeal. Ben's jars were sculpture, pottery designed to have only a single function: to be beautiful— Juliana's own desideratum.

Flattened plates and the thin edges of cups and bowls provided the necessary experience for Ben to make his wide, rimless, thin-walled, and footed bowls. These forms have no obvious visual precedent in Seagrove but come from Korea. Such a bowl must have taken many, many attempts and yet its shape seems both correct and inevitable; that is to say, it is a felicitous shape regardless of its size, amenable to a variety of glazes, whether a

PHOTO 36: ATTRIBUTED TO BEN OWEN OF JUGTOWN POTTERY, **Persian Jar**, *circa 1930s. 17 x 12 inches (43.2 x 30.5 cm). Chinese-blue-glazed stoneware; stamped "Jugtown". Collection of Gallery of Art & Design, North Carolina State University, transfer from the North Carolina Museum of Art, 1998.001.113*

PHOTO 37: ATTRIBUTED TO BEN OWEN OF JUGTOWN POTTERY, **Korean Bowl**, *circa 1930s. 3 x 8½ inches (7.6 x 21.6 cm). Salt-glazed stoneware; decoration by Juliana Busbee. Collection of Gallery of Art & Design, North Carolina State University, transfer from the North Carolina Museum of Art, 1998.001.005*

PHOTO 38: ATTRIBUTED TO BEN OWEN OF JUGTOWN POTTERY, **Korean Bowl with Rim**, *circa 1930s. 3 x 8½ inches (7.6 x 21.6 cm). Salt-glazed stoneware; decoration by Juliana Busbee. Collection of Gallery of Art & Design, North Carolina State University, transfer from the North Carolina Museum of Art, 1998.001.005*

The traditional shapes of pitchers, storage jars, and churns were precedents for pieces like the wine bottle, the Dogwood vase, and the Han vase. Ovoid shapes such as Owen's Grueby jar (a popular type of matte-glazed art pottery) and his Asian-influenced Lily Vase (photo 39), or the ubiquitous egg vase (photo 40) were all art-pottery staples. The new shapes in Jugtown's inventory, like those in C. R. Auman's, contributed to a wider language of form and style. Successful changes were a truly

PHOTO 39: ATTRIBUTED TO BEN OWEN OF JUGTOWN POTTERY, *Left:* **Grueby Jar,** *circa 1930s. 7 x 5½ inches (17.8 x 14 cm). Stoneware; frogskin and salt glaze. Right:* **Lily Vase,** *circa 1930s. 9¼ x 8 inches (23.5 x 20.3 cm). Stoneware; white glaze. Both collection of Gallery of Art & Design, North Carolina State University, transfer from the North Carolina Museum of Art, (left) 1998.001.011; (right) 1998.001.081*

PHOTO 41: UNKNOWN MAKER, **Chinese Storage Jar,** *mid 19th century. 26 x 12 inches (66 x 30.5 cm). Stoneware; embossed, painted. Collection of Gallery of Art & Design, North Carolina State University, transfer from Chinqua Penn Plantation, T2004.005.005*

PHOTO 40: ATTRIBUTED TO BEN OWEN OF JUGTOWN POTTERY, **Egg Vases,** *circa 1930s. Tallest, 4 inches (10.2 cm). Stoneware; (left to right) frogskin, Chinese blue, and Chinese (dogwood) white glazes; all stamped "Jugtown". Collection of Gallery of Art & Design, North Carolina State University, transfer from the North Carolina Museum of Art, (left to right) 1998.001.104, 1998.001.003, 1998.001.124*

salt-glazed piece decorated by Juliana with dogwood petals (photo 37) or an orange earthenware with a tobacco-spit lead glaze. When a raised rim is added to the edge, the bowl has an even stronger profile and a feeling of greater strength (photo 38). The shape welcomes any of the glazes from Jugtown's repertoire; a thickly dripping Chinese blue or a frogskin are equally suited.

Owen and the Busbees limited the number of oriental translations that were made and concentrated on refining them. The Persian jar, for instance, was made only in Chinese blue. Other forms were made in some or all of the limited range of colors, which varied only with the vagaries of the firing process itself.

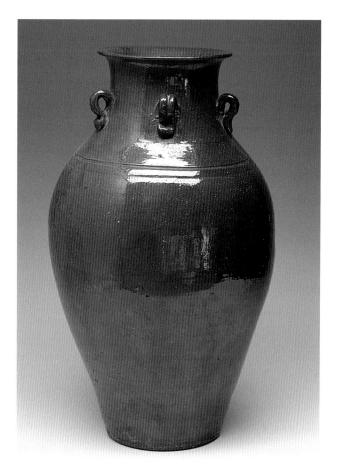

PHOTO 42: JUGTOWN POTTERY, **Vase**, *circa 1950. 25 x 9½ inches (63.5 x 24.1 cm). Earthenware; "tobacco spit" glaze. Collection of Gallery of Art & Design, North Carolina State University, anonymous donor, 1994.009.001*

PHOTO 43: **Jacques and Juliana Busbee living room interior.**

positive process that can be seen and appreciated in the work. A mid-19th-century Chinese storage jar (photo 41, page 49), with its applied decorations, is a crude cousin of an elegant Jugtown piece of a hundred years later (photo 42), whose slender proportions, thinner walls, crisp handles, and strong color are far more appealing than its ancestor. Owen learned much and made what he learned into his own style. At the same time, Owen and his helpers were producing a large amount of useful ware. Production work—making the same form again and again—is a relentless challenge. Jugtown pieces are skilled productions, yet such efforts are masked by the simplicity and elegance of the forms. Ten orange dinner plates or berry bowls or mugs vary only marginally; their differences are not apparent unless they're seen side by side, but such differences don't matter. Indeed, this kind of pottery is a different kind of art, though the potters did not think of themselves as artists but as craftsmen.

Jugtown's work helped the culture of pottery making in the Seagrove area survive. The Busbees' intervention in Seagrove was entrepreneurial, artistic, and in a way, ideological. In 1957, Juliana said that the work done there was "as two hundred years ago."[12] Such assertions along with her decoration of the log cabin in the Colonial Revival style, the way she always greeted visitors as if admitting them to a charmed circle, dining with them before their open fireplace, as if in Colonial times, these were all pure Juliana Busbee (photo 43). After World War II, this vision and its related values were challenged by the same changes that had brought them to Seagrove in the first place.

J. B. COLE POTTERY

"Pottery is no new art; it is the oldest art that we have any record of today. The art of pottery comes to us through the Bible. We have tried to preserve many of the designs that have come down to us from antiquity, for they are still beautiful and their lines graceful and ornamental."

— *J. B. Cole's Pottery catalog, c. 1932*

The Cole pottery catalog sagely promised buyers a reliable inventory of hand-thrown, kiln-fired, colorfast, and waterproof pieces, in any one of 15 colors, made with North Carolina clay. "Orders,"

Cole wrote, "are filled as quickly as possible." And he extended a cordial invitation to visit the pottery any day except Sunday (photo 44).

The first Cole family potter had been Raphard Cole, who worked in Steeds, in Montgomery County. Raphard's son, Evan, fathered J. B., Lorenzo (Wren), and Ruffin (whose son, Charles, eventually established his own pottery). J. B. learned his trade both at home and at several other potteries, including the Hiltons', some 75 miles away in the Catawba Valley. He undoubtedly knew the Aumans, because his brother, Wren, threw clay for C. R., and so probably knew Charles Masten too. The Coles were familiar with Jugtown and other potteries when J. B. decided to open his own place in 1922 (photo 45).

J. B. was smart, energetic, and ambitious. The physical plant he built eschewed all the old ways whenever they could be replaced with more efficient new ones. He ordered glazes from minerals suppliers. He read and learned all he could about preparing and firing clay. The groundhog kiln was replaced with an upright one that permitted him to use saggars—clay containers that protect ware from flying ash and preserve the smooth shiny surfaces of the wares. He was quick to switch his kilns from wood to oil and gas.

PHOTO 44: **J. B. Cole at the treadle wheel, circa 1920s.**
NORTH CAROLINA COLLECTION, PACK MEMORIAL PUBLIC LIBRARY, ASHEVILLE, NORTH CAROLINA

PHOTO 45:
J. B. Cole glazing a piece of ware, circa 1920s.
NORTH CAROLINA COLLECTION, PACK MEMORIAL PUBLIC LIBRARY, ASHEVILLE, NORTH CAROLINA

Potters made wares from late fall until June and farmed in summer until harvest time. The Coles' shop could be reached by the same muddy, rocky, cratered, and rutted dirt roads that characterized the entire region (paved roads weren't built until after World War II). Nevertheless, the business was a thriving one that was hardly slowed by the Depression.

The Coles' success was due to a vision that was more egalitarian than the Busbees' artistic ideals. Although the Cole pottery continued to make some salt-glazed, wood-fired utilitarian stoneware like that made in the 19th century, J. B. seemed to understand that the tourists who traveled east and south to his shop wanted more colorful "art wares" like the ones illustrated in magazines and newspapers. And the Coles warmly welcomed visitors, sometimes inviting them to eat with the family. Tourists could also make suggestions: "These customers would want a fancy pie plate, maybe fluted on the edge, or a casserole or a fancy vase...Neighbors bought it just like the tourist(s)... These northern people...would come and draw for us what they wanted. Then we could change the shape a little, make it more ours" (photo 46).[13]

With such an approach, their business thrived. Sales catalogs offered custom ware and identified its maker, even though it wasn't until the late 20th century that either Nell or Waymon, J. B.'s children, actually signed any pieces (photo 47). The Coles understood that marketing was essential if they were to make the transition from functional to art ware, and they shored up their pottery's pedigree by associating it with antiquity and, in the style of the time, included in the catalog a poem probably inspired by a Bible passage. The Coles learned quickly that regional retailers could market their handmade wares to a clientele that was responsive to the aesthetic ideals of the Colonial Revival, the Arts and Crafts Movement, and the Craft Revival.

To this end, the Coles created the flourishing Sunset Mountain Pottery wholesale line, which they "exported" between 1929 and 1936. Three Asheville businessmen, Hugh C. Brown, Edwin Brown, and W. H. Lashley, sold handcrafted items as part of a wholesale and retail business that had begun in Hugh Brown's downtown Asheville

PHOTO 48: J. B. COLE POTTERY, **Teapot, Dinner Plate, and Small Cup and Saucer,** *circa 1928. Teapot: 7¼ inches (18.4 cm) to handle, 6 inches (15.2 cm) in diameter; plate: 10 inches (25.4 cm) in diameter; cup: 1¾ x 1 inches (4.4 x 2.5 cm); saucer: 2¼ inches (5.7 cm) in diameter. Glazed earthenware; stamped "Sunset Mountain Pottery". Collection of Cynthia and Thomas Edwards*

hardware store. The business grew into a vigorous enterprise with three shops, The Treasure Chest, Log-Cabin, and Three Mountaineers located in Asheville, which was already a significant tourist destination and on its way to becoming a center for the revival of interest in traditional mountain crafts. The Treasure Chest also had stores in New York City, Boston, Chicago, and Los Angeles. Brochures and magazine advertisements for their handcrafted, "mountain-made" pottery announced that the makers drew their inspiration from the beautiful colors found in the mountain landscapes and seasons (photo 48).

A Three Mountaineers sales folio (photo 49) proclaimed that "Pottery making is generally conceded to be about the oldest art known to man—yet today it is just as fascinating and interesting as ever—/Sunset Mountain Pottery is one of the few lines still being made by hand… on an old-fashioned 'kick' wheel, the power being furnished by the stout left foot, and the finger markings left by the potter's hands show clearly on the graceful contours of each piece…"

Hugh Brown traveled east and visited the Coles on several occasions to buy their "mountain-made" work. Other dealers from outside North

PHOTO 47:
Waymon Cole at the wheel.
NORTH CAROLINA COLLECTION, UNIVERSITY OF NORTH CAROLINA LIBRARY AT CHAPEL HILL

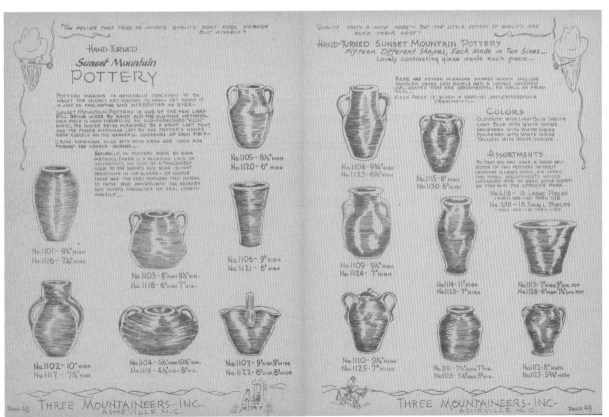

PHOTO 49: **"Hand Turned Sunset MountainPottery".**
NORTH CAROLINA COLLECTION, PACK MEMORIAL PUBLIC LIBRARY, ASHEVILLE, NORTH CAROLINA

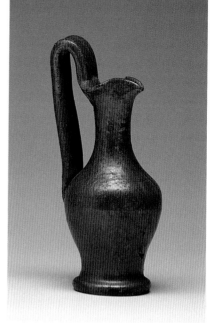

PHOTO 50: J. B. COLE POTTERY, **Two Vases,** *circa 1930s.*
Left: 6½ x 6½ inches (16.5 x 16.5 cm); right: 8½ x 9½ inches (21.6 x 24.1 cm).
Both earthenware; chrome red glaze; (left) ink stamped "Shamburger's Handmade,
RFD Richmond"; (right) paper label reads "Daison Ware, American Handmade,
The Hecht Co., Washington, D. C., $2.50". Gallery of Art & Design, North
Carolina State University, gift of the Friends of the Gallery Collectors Circle, (left)
1999.026.002; (right) 2001.014.002

PHOTO 51: J. B. COLE POTTERY,
Rebecca Pitcher, *circa 1930s.*
Height, 6 inches (15.2 cm). Glazed
earthenware. Collection of Cynthia
and Thomas Edwards

Carolina also kept the pottery busy. They supplied wares to the Shamburger Department Store in Richmond; Hecht's, in Washington, D.C., sold it as "Daison Ware" (photo 50). The North State Pottery in Sanford, for example, sold over half their production outside North Carolina. The J. B. Cole stamp is particularly rare because wholesalers liked to apply their own paper labels and ink stamps; they did not want to disclose the sources of their merchandise.

The 1932 Cole catalog offered 524 pieces in many sizes and colors. Tall floor vases and globular vases, two-handled vases and wide plates alluded to forms that were their immediate ancestors: churns, chamber pots, and "dirt dishes," a common, local way of referring to earthenware for the table and the kitchen. There were also exotic forms like the Rebecca Pitcher (photo 51), so named because it was probably adapted from a Biblical illustration of the story of Rebecca at the well.

PHOTO 52: J. B.
COLE POTTERY,
Vase, *circa 1930s.*
5½ x 5¾ inches
(14 x 14.6 cm).
Glazed earthenware;
stamped "Sunset
Mountain Pottery".
Collection of Gallery
of Art & Design,
North Carolina
State University, gift
of Cynthia and
Thomas Edwards in
memory of
Douglas Blount,
2002.043.001

A globelike Sunset Mountain Pottery vase (photo 52) is enhanced with heavy throwing rings (i.e., circular marks made by the potter's hand that hadn't been smoothed away) and an opaque light-aqua glaze that disguised the clay body beneath it. It's small enough to handle and pack easily, and its shape and the telltale rings recall metal Art Deco ware. The Sunset Mountain glaze palette included clear green, dense white, cobalt blue, yellow, pink, red, dark purple, and a dark, mottled green. Though the ware is generally heavy, the body's density doesn't prevent the rims, handles, spouts, and other features from being well articulated: clear, clean, firmly attached, and carefully made.

PHOTO 53: J. B. COLE, **Apothecary Jars,** *1930s. Largest, 8 x 8¼ inches (20.3 x 21 cm). Earthenware; various glazes. Collection of Cynthia and Thomas Edwards*

Other Cole pottery pieces, such as the two earthenware vases shown in photo 50, are light and thin-walled. The then-popular chrome red glaze with strong black striations enhances these relatively small vases. The smaller one rises from a dainty foot that is echoed in its thin lip. The three thin, pulled handles that rim the neck of the taller piece animate its shoulders.

The Coles made globular, wide-mouthed vases (photo 53) adapted from a traditional apothecary jar form. In its best realizations, the form's proportions are perfect—the opening not too large, the shoulder exactly the right scale to support a wide neck. The handles were made from a single rolled piece of clay split down the center, and though they're attached, the handles seem to be extensions of the articulated throwing rings; they are at one with the body. Each of the glaze colors takes advantage of the form's undulations and details in different ways. Such skill reinforces the impression that a sensitive human being made each vase, one by one (photo 54).

A nearly mirror-image pair of earthenware vases may represent the epitome of the Cole aesthetic (photo 55). Their thin, smooth trumpet bells are like that of a musical instrument and at the same time naturalistic, like squash or cucumber blossoms without any ridges. Applied handles, rolled very thin, animate the form quite like the gesture of a person whose hands are stretching to his neck. Such work is a unique combination of fineness, strong color, and shape.

PHOTO 54: J. B. COLE POTTERY, **Apothecary Jars,** *circa 1930s. Left: 8 x 6½ inches (20.3 x 16.5 cm) at base; right: 5 x 4½ inches (12.7 x 11.4 cm) at base. Earthenware; various glazes. Collection of Cynthia and Thomas Edwards*

PHOTO 55: J. B. COLE, **Pair of Trumpet Vases,** *circa 1930s. Each, 4 x 5⅛ inches (10.2 x 13 cm) at bell. Earthenware; chrome yellow glaze. Collection of Gallery of Art & Design, North Carolina State University, gift of the Friends of the Gallery Collectors Circle, 2003.016.001A&B*

PHOTO 56: J. B. COLE, **Elephant Pitcher,** *circa 1930s. 16½ x 8½ inches (41.9 x 21.6 cm). Earthenware; aqua glaze. Collection of Gallery of Art & Design, North Carolina State University, gift of Ann Roth and John Coffey, 2000.027.001*

The Cole catalog of 1932, a wish book in a time of wish books, only hints at the magnitude of work they made. The Coles and their numerous helpers must have produced between 30,000 and 50,000 pieces annually. And despite the technological processes they employed, many pairs of hands handled each pot. So little functional ware has survived from this period that it is likely the Cole Pottery's production concentrated on decorative wares instead (photo 56).

The Coles continued to work some during the Second World War, but the rationing of minerals affected glazes and thus production. After the war, they lost no time filling the barnlike shop near Steeds. J. B.'s children, Waymon and Nell, were essential to the success of the Cole pottery (photo 57). After J. B.'s death, they ran the business with Nell's husband, Philmore Graves, and Bascomb King, another local potter, until Nell closed it in the late 1990s.

A HAZY FUTURE

In 1950, North Carolina was poised to move forward into the second half of the 20th century. The state's recovery from the Depression was fueled by the construction and growth of military bases: Fort Bragg at Fayetteville; Cherry Point, with its air base and facilities for the rebuilding and repair of airplanes near New Bern; and Camp Lejeune, near Jacksonville, all provided substantial opportunities for the building industry and created a larger population with disposable income. Most manufacturing continued as part of the war effort; furniture manufacturers in the western part of the state converted their plants to make wooden parts for airplanes.

Soldiers returned to jobs in the factories, mills, and on family farms; many also used the GI bill to enter colleges and universities that would not have been accessible to them in pre-war years, creating a new, larger class of university educated managers, lawyers, doctors, teachers, architects, and bankers. The distance the state had traveled since the beginning of the century could be measured in a hundred ways: growth of nonrural populations, increased numbers of children in school (and for more days), more miles of paved roads and train rails, larger networks of electrical power, and extensive rural electrification.

The 1950s stretched ahead as a time of promise, continued advancement, and personal well-being for North Carolinians. Unfair labor practices were challenged before the war, but the state's resistance to labor unions and its accompanying strife were swept away by the approaching war. The complex and seemingly intractable problems of a deeply racist society embedded in the state's laws and traditions remained hidden by apparent postwar prosperity. The changing nature of agriculture, with fewer farms, reliance on share-cropping and tenancy, and subsequent poverty, was also a nascent challenge to the traditionally rural, agricultural state. The idea of a new South, which had emerged in the 19th century, persisted, but the meaning of the term in the 20th century was yet to be discovered. The potteries in the Seagrove area had already undergone one transformation.

The successful conversion from the seasonal production of functional wares—mostly marketed locally to a rural agricultural society—to year-round activity marketed regionally to a consumer-driven society, was accomplished well before the beginning of World War II. Not only in the Seagrove area, but in nearby Sanford and its surroundings, potters who persisted and changed

PHOTO 57:
Nell Cole Graves throwing a vase.
NORTH CAROLINA COLLECTION, UNIVERSITY OF NORTH CAROLINA LIBRARY AT CHAPEL HILL

THE WARES FROM THE SEAGROVE AREA WERE TRULY LOCAL, WITH AUTHENTIC HISTORICAL ROOTS

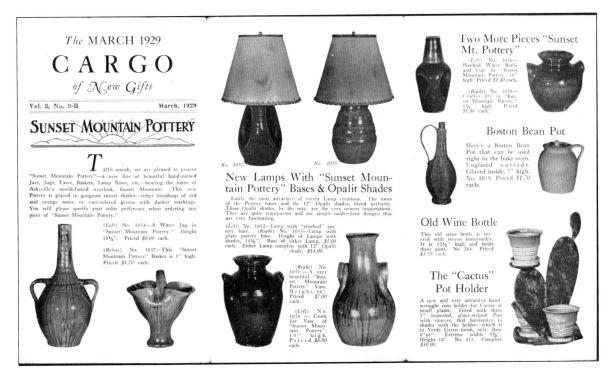

PHOTO 58:
March 1929 Cargo, update of the catalogs of traveling salesmen working for the Treasure Chest, showing Sunset Mountain Pottery.
NORTH CAROLINA COLLECTION, PACK MEMORIAL PUBLIC LIBRARY, ASHEVILLE, NORTH CAROLINA

were able to maintain viable businesses. The outer trappings of tradition—handmade, lead-glazed, wood-fired earthenware and salt-glazed stoneware, and the labor-intensive work it required—still depended on a network of family and local journeymen potters. Family potteries like those of J. B. Cole and Melvin Owens were joined by entrepreneurs such as Jacques and Juliana Busbee, C. R. Auman, and Rebecca and John Cooper, who founded North State Pottery near Sanford. They supplied capital, marketing ideas, and a willingness and ability to reach out to the wider world. Magazines and tourists provided ideas for changes in the appearance and types of the new ware. Pottery makers in the Catawba Valley and around Asheville, like Oscar L. Bachelder, sought ways to create new and saleable wares (photo 58, page 57).

Between 1900 and 1950, all the potters responded to an aesthetic with work that was suitable for Cape Cod–style houses and Arts and Crafts–style bungalows that filled suburbs. While the architecture and furniture recalled aspects of a shared, generic American past, the wares from the Seagrove area were truly local, with authentic historical roots (photo 60). The survival of the potters and their products was due to their desire to preserve a habitual way of life in which pottery making was fully integrated. And they did it. Even C. R. Auman's failure contained some of the key elements of success: experimentation, marketing, capital, good potters, and strong, beautiful work. The lesson to be learned, perhaps, was that the production of some utilitarian and tablewares was essential to survival.

The most notable fact about Seagrove in 1950 was that a few potteries were still in operation; a new generation of future potters might choose to take up the challenge of surviving as full-time potters. By this time, the work that had been fresh in 1925 or 1935 seemed outdated, and traditional salt-glazed stoneware—the foundation of the Seagrove-area potters' livelihood—was at least a generation past.

THE LESSON TO BE LEARNED, PERHAPS, WAS THAT THE PRODUCTION OF SOME UTILITARIAN AND TABLEWARES WAS ESSENTIAL TO SURVIVAL.

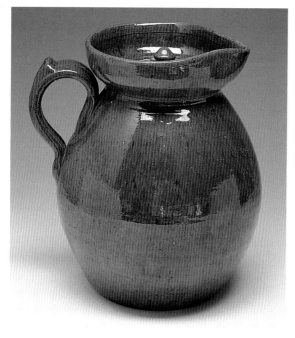

Baxter Welch's pottery shop near Harper's Crossroads in Chatham County, circa 1900

NOTES

1 The Arts and Crafts Movement promoted the tenet that art helped create a good life. For more on this subject, see Wendy Kaplan, *The Art That Is Life* (see Bibliography).

2 Also spelled Mitchfield, this area north of Seagrove was one of the largest cleared fields in the area. It was named for a person named Mitchel, nicknamed Mitch.

3 Thirteen Auman pieces acquired by the Newark Museum have a few paper labels that identify Auman as their maker. Fortuitously, the museum's purchase was accompanied by a 1927 receipt from the seller, Clay Crafters of New York City. Despite considerable research by many persons, nothing is known about the Clay Crafters business.

4 Dorothy Auman quoted in Sweezy, *Raised In Clay*, 28.

5 Masten, a dry cleaner and dyer from Bloomington, Indiana, had become interested in ceramics, especially glazing. For at least one summer, probably in 1927, he studied ceramics in New York, probably at The New York State School of Clayworking and Ceramics at Alfred University.

6 Although the company emptied the large vein, a few deposits of clay can still be found in the vicinity.

7 Douglas DeNatale's essay on the Busbees (see Bibliography) is probably the best discussion, to date, of the context and cultural milieu in which the Busbees lived and from which they derived their enthusiasm for North Carolina pottery and the business that followed.

8 In 1957, Juliana wrote to the artist Harvey K. Littleton, who had not yet moved to North Carolina, "It will be so nice to have you and your friend visit Jugtown. There is an extra wheel here and two kilns, one for stoneware and the white pots. Remember the work done here is as it was two hundred years ago." Archives of American Art, Harvey K. Littleton Papers. www.aaa.si.edu

9 The roles of both the Arts and Crafts Movement and the Colonial Revival in the renewal of Southern handcrafts were crucial in this period. The Southern Highland Craft Guild was founded in 1926 and the Penland School of Crafts in 1929. These western North Carolina organizations (and others in Southern Appalachia) were part of a wide movement that brought settlement and industrial schools to impoverished mountain dwellers, encouraging them to continue or to revive traditional handcrafts as a means to supplement their incomes; both schools taught children and young people. See also Eaton's *Handicrafts of the Southern Appalachian Highlands,* which tells of the success of this movement and also credits the Jugtown Pottery as an important source of the survival of traditional ceramics. Eaton wrote that the Busbees mirrored the same ideals as those that prevailed in the western part of the state.

10 The "jugtown" name was not unique; any pottery-producing area might be so nicknamed. In North Carolina, a Catawba Valley post office was named Jugtown in 1874, and another Jugtown was located in the western region, in Buncombe County.

11 Gay M. Hertzman, in her essay on the Busbees (see Bibliography), describes the role Asian and Middle Eastern influences played in their vision. Ben Owen III also has drawings made by his grandfather in the Metropolitan and other museums.

12 Archives of American Art, Harvey K. Littleton Papers. www.aaa.si.edu

13 Sweezy, *Raised In Clay,* 177.

CHAPTER 3

SOUTHERN MATERIAL CULTURE & THE DISCOVERY OF SEAGROVE

PHOTO 31: BEN OWEN III, **Korean Bowl,** *1983*

"We found Mrs. Juliana Busbee, one of the founders of Jugtown, there alone that day, the gift shop locked and no one working. But she came from her house, greeted us graciously, and led us on a tour of the place. ...I was hooked, right then, I now realize,"

—*Beth Thompson*

B eth Thompson first visited Seagrove in 1950. Her warm, candid memoir recounts tales of the potters and their stories, and the frequent visits she, her family, and friends made there for more than 40 years. She also bought wares from M. L. Owens, Jugtown, Ben Owen senior's Old Plank Road Pottery, the Aumans' Seagrove Pottery, and Zedith Teague (near Robbins), but mostly she bought from J. B. Cole's pottery near Seagrove and from A. R. Cole, C. C. Cole's brother, in Sanford. Forty-five years later, Thompson realized "My shelves were full and my surfaces covered…It was time to quit…Besides, the old potters from whom I had been buying my pieces were no longer on the scene. My sources were no more."

Thompson's husband had relocated his family from Iowa after being hired by North Carolina State College, which was at the heart of a statewide industrial and agricultural expansion.

PHOTO 1: **J. S. Dorton, in front of his namesake arena, Matthew Nowicki and William Henry Deitrick, architects, North Carolina State Fairgrounds, Raleigh, 1950–1952.** COURTESY OF THE NORTH CAROLINA STATE ARCHIVES NORTH CAROLINA DEPARTMENT OF ARCHIVES AND HISTORY, N.93.3.9

THE POTTERIES NEEDED TO BE DESTINATIONS THEMSELVES, NOT JUST STOPS ON THE WAY TO SOMEWHERE ELSE

In 1952, not far from the campus, the J. S. Dorton Arena at the State Fairgrounds was dedicated. Named in honor of the fair manager who had risked hiring a young Polish émigré architect, Matthew Nowicki, to design the building, it is now internationally recognized as one of the icons of modernism in American architecture and design. The building represents Dorton's desire to demonstrate the state's move toward progressivism (photo 1).

At the same time, in New Bern, the former colonial capitol, "Tryon's Palace" (at one time the governor's house) was being restored. The late Georgian building (photo 2), designed by the English architect John Hawkes and built between 1767 and 1770, is in stark contrast to the arena, yet the two are representative of the two huge forces that drove postwar North Carolina: a powerful allegiance to the past and the intense desire for progress. Even the university expansion that brought the Thompsons to Raleigh was part of North Carolina's look to the future.

PHOTO 2: **John Hawkes, architect, "Tryon's Palace," New Bern, North Carolina, 1767–1770, restored by William Muirhead Construction Company, beginning 1950.** COURTESY OF THE NORTH CAROLINA STATE ARCHIVES NORTH CAROLINA DEPARTMENT OF ARCHIVES AND HISTORY, N.64.4.3

EXHIBITIONS AND
PUBLICATIONS ABOUT
THE POTTERS AND
THEIR WAY OF LIFE
BEGAN TO RAISE
THE HISTORICAL
AND CULTURAL
CONSCIOUSNESS OF
THE NATION.

The countryside they enjoyed so much on their trips to Seagrove seemed virtually unaffected by those powerful economic and cultural forces, but in the period between the world wars, up until 1980, North Carolina's urban population had actually doubled, to 50 percent. Of those who remained in rural areas, many had abandoned farming and begun commuting to jobs in industry. In the span of 30 years, 5,000 manufacturing plants were built, mostly in the Piedmont. Returning GIs swelled the state's university system, growing numbers of graduates staffed the many new businesses, and increasing numbers of children filled still-segregated public school systems. Such economic stimulation eventually paved country roads, widened secondary roads, and turned two-lane highways into four. This general climate of prosperity and optimism created many potential buyers for pottery.

PHOTO 3: **Bayard Wootten, Weavers Cabin at Penland. This cabin at the crest of Conley's Ridge, in Penland, North Carolina, was built by families in the vicinity and is an important center for that widely scattered community. It was in this cabin that the meeting was held out of which the Southern Highland Craft Guild grew.**

PHOTO 4: **Flat Top Manor at the Moses H. Cone Memorial Park, Blue Ridge Parkway.**
COURTESY OF THE NORTH CAROLINA DEPARTMENT OF COMMERCE, DIVISION OF TOURISM, FILM AND SPORTS DEVELOPMENT

Around Seagrove, the evolving nature of the economy and the culture required its potters to continue to balance tradition with opportunity. As tourism grew and wholesale pottery businesses expanded, the potters realized that it was essential to find ways to attract more people to the area. The potteries needed to be destinations themselves, not just stops on the way to somewhere else.

THE HISTORY OF PLACE

The Colonial Revival and the Arts and Crafts Movement stimulated the study of traditional crafts before the Second World War and publications like Allen H. Eaton's late-1930s *Handicrafts of the Southern Highlands* documented its makers (photo 3). The marketing efforts of the Southern Highland Craft Guild offered tourists the best of work in sites located along the Blue Ridge Parkway like Flat Top Manor on the Cone Estate near Blowing Rock, North Carolina (photo 4). Similar to Bascom Lamar Lunsford's field recordings of Appalachian folk music made in 1928, Eaton's work took on renewed significance during the nation's post-World War II years of recovery.

Everything American gained in importance; academic attention focused on American history and the academic disciplines of folklore and folk life were developed, ready to document and preserve the American experience in all its forms. In 1960, Ralph Rinzler, who became the Smithsonian's premier folklorist, followed Lunsford's lead and studied and recorded folk music in the Southern Appalachian Highlands. He found that traditional music and its makers still abounded, along with many kinds of skilled craftspeople, including weavers and potters. Rinzler's efforts inspired young scholars to study traditional craftspeople all over the South. Tennessee's Carter family and North Carolina's Doc Watson came to the fore, along with those other great Southern contributions to American music, jazz, and the blues. And as their visual counterparts, the folk potters of the South also emerged as subjects worthy of study. The Bicentennial Year added impetus to the interest just as the Centennial of 1876 had done.

Exhibitions and publications about the potters and their way of life began to raise the historical and cultural consciousness of the nation. Nancy

Sweezy's *Raised in Clay: The Southern Folk Pottery Tradition* and Charles G. Zug III's *Turners and Burners: The Folk Potters of North Carolina* ensured that North Carolina's folk potters would not be forgotten. Their timing was impeccable, as these books celebrated a way of life rooted in a rural agricultural society just as that society was beginning to vanish. At about the same time, museum exhibitions helped expand knowledge of defunct and contemporary potteries. Between about 1980 and 1995, eight or more North Carolina shows presented traditional work by Seagrove-area potters and made scholarly inquiries into the nature of the relationship between past and present.

THE ASCENDANCY OF CONTEMPORARY CRAFT

Perhaps as significant as the documentation of folk potters was the transformation of the idea of craft itself. Postwar, many GIs entered design schools whose curricula included designing functional wares, furniture, houses, apparel, and automobiles. Schools like Cranbrook in Michigan and Black Mountain College in North Carolina encouraged cross-disciplinary studies. They invited craftspeople like the distinguished potter Shoji Hamada and his British adherent Bernard Leach to discuss and describe the roles of craft and craft education as means to enriching and countering the growing materialism of America since World War II. Craft objects—glass, furniture, ceramics, textiles—might be designed and manufactured in factories, but they could also be produced in studios by academically trained makers. Penland School of Crafts in North Carolina and Haystack Mountain School of Crafts in Maine, among others, provided high-level summer programs taught by emerging craft professionals.

The birth of studio craft, as it came to be called, occurred at about the same time that consumers became interested in acquiring and collecting one-of-a-kind, handmade, and historical folk art, which soon grew to include contemporary craft. Historical folk art could be seen in collections such as the Abby Aldrich Rockefeller Folk Art Collection at Colonial Williamsburg and in the newly created Folk Art Museum in New York City. Fueled by Bicentennial fervor and a host of conflicting ideological issues, which included civil rights, the back-to-the-land movement, and widespread disenchantment with the Vietnam War, craft and the life of craftspeople seemed to represent a more authentic America. Moreover, objects made by craftspeople, unlike contemporary American painting and sculpture, were more affordable, and they seemed to relate to a past that could be more easily appreciated than the literal and theoretical abstractions of fine art. The efflorescence of a truly American art in abstract expressionism and its successors appeared to many as art for the wealthy, while the expressive and purely sculptural ceramic work of Peter Voulkos obviously had its roots in pottery and was—at that time—less costly (photo 5).

Studio pottery aesthetics threw into high relief the great differences between the modern craft movement and the history and traditions of a place like Seagrove. American studio potters knew little of their own history or traditions and there were few if any resources (such as established, art-historical disciplines of study) to help them learn it. Meanwhile, the potters of Seagrove learned, as

PHOTO 5: PETER VOULKOS, **Rocking Pot**, *1956. 13⅜ x 21 x 17½ inches (34.6 x 53.3 x 44.6 cm). Stoneware. Smithsonian American Art Museum, Washington, DC/Art Resource NY*

they always had, from within their own families and by working for other area potters. Their inspirations were as varied as that of the studio potters; however, their goals weren't to achieve personal expression but rather to make functional, affordable wares.

These separate but related developments—the creation of a modern historical consciousness and the documentation of an endangered traditional way of life and work—ultimately reshaped the practice of pottery in the Seagrove area. The contemporary American craft movement added another stream of energy and creativity that the potters in the Seagrove area could draw from as their working world continued to change.

AUMAN'S SEAGROVE POTTERY SHOP

Just as a miniature whiskey jug might symbolize the early 20th century's market shift from self-sufficiency to consumerism, the small bowl shown in photo 6 represents some part of Seagrove's struggle, decades later, to promote itself as a tourist destination. Dorothy and Walter Auman (photo 7), self-appointed public relations and marketing agents for the Seagrove potters as well as ardent local historians, archaeologists, and pottery collectors, thanked North Carolina politician and advocate of craft Hargrove (Skipper) Bowles with this tangible reminder of Seagrove's central role in tourism.[1] It also has the trademarks of Auman earthenware. It is a simple, well-thrown form. Its cogglewheel decoration, made by rolling a wheel along the clay's surface, focuses attention on the surface's warm colors.

Dorothy Cole Auman was the daughter of C. C. (Charles) Cole, who ran a pottery production shop but was not himself a potter.[2] A descendant of generations of potters (Nell Cole Graves was her cousin), Dorothy wanted to make pottery from early childhood. As did Graves, she persisted until her father asked Wren Cole to teach her. Dorothy learned quickly. During her younger years she had seen traditional, functional, salt-glazed stoneware replaced by large, attractive, and brightly colored earthenware planters, floor vases, umbrella stands, and a variety of smaller pieces, which sold well to the new market (photo 8).

PHOTO 7: **Dorothy and Walter Auman, late 1980s.**
COURTESY OF WALTER S. AUMAN, JR.

PHOTO 6: DOROTHY AND WALTER AUMAN, **Bowl,** *circa 1969. 6½ inches (16.5 cm) in diameter. Glazed earthenware; cogglewheel border; inscribed "Seagrove Pottery, Skipper 1969–1970" on the bottom. Collection of Gallery of Art & Design, North Carolina State University, gift of Tandy Solomon, 2000.040.001b*

PHOTO 8: ATTRIBUTED TO WAYMON COLE, **Pair of Floor Vases,** *circa 1940. 15¼ x 11 inches (38.7 x 27.9 cm). Earthenware; bright aqua glaze. Collection of Gallery of Art & Design, North Carolina State University, gift of the Friends of the Gallery Collectors Circle, 2000.020.003a & b*

PHOTO 11: **Walter Auman in the Seagrove Pottery Shop, circa 1960s.** COURTESY OF WALTER S. AUMAN, JR.

Dorothy started by making baskets, vases, and miniatures. While the traditional storage jars and churns had been great precedents for floor vases and umbrella stands, her smaller pieces were sometimes derived from magazines and books, and from the suggestions of tourists and patrons. Dorothy said many times that outsiders were very important to the survival of successful pottery production because they brought fresh ideas and bought wares.

In 1949, Dorothy married Walter Auman and in 1952, he came to work for C. C. Cole. Making pottery for the wholesale market required concentration and hard work, and it was stressful. A crew of three or four potters working steadily could average production of 3,000 pots a day. A big oil kiln that held 5,000 pieces was fired twice a week and one of the other oil kilns was fired every day. Honey and syrup jugs, destined for truck shipment to Knoxville, Tennessee, and Winchester, Virginia, made up a large part of the Cole shop's production. When this market dried up, C. C. developed another outlet, the Carolina Soap and Candle Company. Miniature cream and sugar bowls with a matte green glaze, filled with wax and a wick, became souvenir candles (photo 9). Cole's potters also made a jug with pierced sides, called a manger lantern, and three sizes of candle cups. Other small decorative accessories aimed at the tourist trade included planters, ashtrays, and cigarette and match holders (photo 10).

PHOTO 10: C. C. COLE, *nd. Left:* **Ashtray.** *7 inches (17.8 cm) in diameter. Earthenware; brown glaze; stamped "C. C. Cole Pottery". Center:* **Bowl.** *3 x 4¾ inches (7.6 x 12 cm). Earthenware; brown glaze; stamped "C.C. Cole Pottery". Right:* **Vase.** *4 x 4 inches (10.2 x 10.2 cm). Earthenware; Swirlware; clear lead glaze. All, collection of Gallery of Art & Design, North Carolina State University, (left and center) gifts of the Friends of the Gallery Collectors Circle, 2002.020.012, 2002.020.016, respectively; (right) gift of Barry and Allen Huffman, 2002.048.001*

PHOTO 9: C. C. COLE POTTERY, **Miniature Creamer and Sugar Bowl,** *nd. Each, 2½ x 2½ inches (6.4 x 6.4 cm). Wax-filled earthenware; matte green glaze; "Carolina Soap and Candle Company" sticker. Collection of Gallery of Art & Design, North Carolina State University, gift of the Friends of the Gallery Collectors Circle, 73*

PHOTO 12: **Dorothy Auman at the wheel, Seagrove Pottery Shop, October 1987.**
PHOTO © DOWARD NIXON JONES, JR.

PHOTO 13: SEAGROVE POTTERY, **Pair of Candlesticks and Teapot,** *1982–1986. Candlesticks: 7 inches (17.8 cm) tall; teapot: 7½ x 6 inches (19 x 15.2 cm). Earthenware; "stone blue" glaze. Collection of Gallery of Art & Design, North Carolina State University, Leonidas J. Betts Collection, (candlesticks) 19991.22.118A&B; (teapot) 1991.22.113*

In 1953, the Aumans bought land and built a workshop and sales shop of their own, although they also worked for C. C. until his death in 1967. They named their wares "Seagrove Pottery" (photo 11). In this new phase, the Aumans wanted to focus on making their own pottery, explore the history of the area, and publicize the Seagrove potters' heritage. Within a few years, their efforts began to bear fruit.

Dorothy threw and Walter glazed, making work that was consistently domestic in form, feeling, and purpose (photo 12). Fluted service pieces and batter bowls with tall pulled handles, casseroles, pie plates, and vases made up part of the repertoire. Candlesticks with a "stone blue" glaze (Dorothy named it so because of the glaze's slatelike qualities) are almost too simple and direct; they have no inner rims to actually hold candles (photo 13), but the design itself is elegant. The Aumans made versatile straight-sided bowls that might hold water for a dog or flower arrangements (photo 14). The old familiar milk crock had become a planter large enough to hold a clay flowerpot.

Dorothy once observed that she never saw a teapot among any 19th-century Seagrove wares, but she and Walter created a distinctive teapot for their customers. Seagrove Pottery's soft and unassuming

PHOTO 14: SEAGROVE POTTERY, **Two Sauce Boats, Vase, and Straight-Sided Bowl,** *circa 1980s. Straight-sided bowl: 3 x 6¾ inches (7.6 x 17.1 cm); large sauce boat: 3 x 4 inches (7.6 x 10.2 cm); small sauce boat: 2½ x 3 inches (6.4 x 7.6 cm); vase: 8½ x 4 inches (21.6 x 10.2 cm). Earthenware; matte green glaze, yellow matte glaze. Collection of Gallery of Art & Design, North Carolina State University, (bowl) 1992.15.020; (sauce boats) gift of the College of Wooster, Ohio, 1992.15.020b and c; (vase) Leonidas J. Betts Collection, 1991.22.117*

mid-century palette (matte yellows, greens, browns, and the stone blue glaze) and the work's simple and innate elegance were perfectly suited for the home. Dorothy sometimes used slip to paint flowers or other decorations on the earthenware. Auman pottery was hand-signed "Seagrove, NC" or "Seagrove Pottery" on the bottom.

Dorothy regretted that she never had the time to make salt-glazed stoneware, which would have required building a separate kiln in which to fire it. Still, there was plenty of work, so the Aumans accepted apprentices and trained several potters

steps to secure the future of the Museum and within a few years they sold the collection to the Mint Museum in Charlotte.

Nevertheless, the Aumans remained Seagrove promoters. They helped start the first Seagrove Pottery Festival (in 1982), organized the first North Carolina Pottery Conference in 1987 (in Randolph County), and were among the founders of the North Carolina Pottery Center, which opened in 1998. They also encouraged the area's younger potters and urged new ones to come to Seagrove.

"IT IS NOT HOW MUCH IS TURNED IN A DAY'S WORK, BUT HOW BEAUTIFULLY,"

—*Juliana Busbee*

in their shop, including Robert Armfield, who soon opened his own pottery, and Joe Wilkinson, who decided not to become a potter but used the expertise he gained there to become an important pottery historian.

As the Aumans saw their wholesale profits shrink, they looked to new avenues of income. Beginning in the early 1950s, Dorothy and Walter exhibited at the Village of Yesteryear, a large hall at the annual state fair in Raleigh, the capital. There, alongside wood carvers, basket makers, weavers, quilters, and makers of traditional musical instruments, the Aumans demonstrated throwing and sold their ceramics.

The Aumans also collected Seagrove wares from the 19th and early 20th centuries. In 1969, they moved the Asheboro and Aberdeen Railroad depot onto their property and opened the Seagrove Potters Museum in it (photo 15, page 71). The museum showed examples of ceramics from other parts of the state and work by contemporary potters. The museum became a mecca for many collectors and potters alike. Dorothy was often asked to identify work from the area, which encouraged her to continue her informal scholarship on the subject. When she was diagnosed with breast cancer in 1980, the couple decided to take

Tragically, the Aumans were killed in a 1991 automobile accident, and with their deaths, the Seagrove potters lost great champions. Lost also was Dorothy's knowledge and insight into the complex potting past that she and Walter were connected to by birth. This knowledge, Ralph Rinzler has lamented, should have been a vital part of the contemporary pottery movement, but those makers took their models from European and Asian sources instead.

Due to the scholarship of the Aumans and various folk historians, the importance of Seagrove as a locus of traditional Southern pottery unlike any other began to gain currency. The Aumans had been keenly aware of how little was known of Seagrove's 19th-century work, and of the history of Southern pottery production in general. For a long time, historians and collectors had ignored the place precisely because of the area's stylistic diversity and the assumption that some potters had catered to popular taste. Ultimately, Rinzler and other historians doing similar research were catalysts for an explosion of information that followed in the 1980s and 1990s, as people not only studied the folk pottery of the South, but in the process rediscovered the art pottery of the Arts and Crafts Movement.

JUGTOWN: TRANSFORMATIONS

While Dorothy and Walter Auman were producing thousands of pots for wholesale at C. C. Cole's, Juliana Busbee was struggling to keep Jugtown open (photo 16). Jacques had died in 1947, and she increasingly relied on Ben Owen, Jugtown's master potter, to oversee the entire pottery operation. He not only threw ware—a full-time job in itself—but also bought supplies, packed orders, and ran the sales shop. Meanwhile, in her campaign to ensure that the state and the nation did not forget Jugtown, Juliana traveled, wrote, and lectured about the pottery and the role the two of them had played in "saving" a traditional American craft. In honor of her husband, she also arranged exhibitions of Jugtown work in memory of Jacques Busbee. Even though the pottery was in an increasingly precarious state, Juliana proudly claimed that

Jugtown had never been run as a profit-making enterprise and so they never kept any records. "It is not how much is turned in a day's work, but how beautifully," she told one writer.

Nevertheless, the business had to support Juliana, Ben Owen, his wife and two children, and a few employees. Equipment upkeep was constant and sometimes sales were slow and uneven. In addition, Jugtown was threatened by a more acute issue: would the pottery continue after Juliana's death?

In 1958, a small group of concerned museum and academic people, including Ben Williams from the North Carolina Museum of Art and John Allcott, who taught art history at UNC-Chapel Hill, together created the nonprofit "Jugtown Incorporated" to manage Jugtown and to provide for Juliana's care.[3] At the end of 1958, Juliana

PHOTO 16: **Jacques and Juliana Busbee outside the Jugtown sales shop, about 1940.**
COURTESY OF PAM AND VERNON OWENS, JUGTOWN

agreed to the arrangement and deeded Jugtown to the corporation. The group hoped that the state of North Carolina could be persuaded to take over Jugtown after Juliana's death. But the relationship between the corporation and Ben Owen was unclear, and in the absence of any type of agreement, Ben announced that he was leaving Jugtown, first in January, then March, of 1959. Ben was the essential ingredient for the pottery's future, and the intervention of the corporation undoubtedly threw his role into limbo.

Then, to the complete surprise of Jugtown Incorporated, a contract was signed between Juliana Busbee and John Maré that formed the "Jacques and Juliana Busbee's Jugtown, Incorporated." Maré was a New Yorker who had established his home in Southern Pines some 10 years earlier. Their intention was to preserve the pottery as a working business; Juliana was to remain in the house and Maré would provide her a monthly stipend. Juliana signed a deed giving the property to the new corporation. Now two deeds were held by two different corporations; Juliana apparently did not remember signing either one.

John Maré took over as Jugtown's manager in April and Ben Owen left shortly afterward, moving up the road to a house on Highway 705—the Old Plank Road—where he opened his own pottery. Jugtown closed, and the nonprofit Jugtown, Incorporated, sued unsuccessfully to have Maré's agreement nullified. Jugtown remained in the control of Maré and Juliana's corporation, and the court confirmed that contract in 1960.

When Jugtown reopened in the spring of 1960, Juliana was still living in her house. Maré began physical improvements to the buildings and the grounds, and he hired Vernon, the 19-year-old son of M. L. (Melvin) Owens, as Jugtown's new potter. Ben Owen's departure—like Maré's involvement—caused a lot of discussion, some of it critical of Maré. The situation left tension in the air.

PHOTO 15: **Interior of Potters Museum, circa 1978.**

COURTESY MINT MUSEUM OF ART, CHARLOTTE, NORTH CAROLINA

Country Roads

Although there were potters who were older and more experienced, Maré had chosen a young Owens to be the operator of a pottery with a statewide reputation. The choice of Vernon, Ben Owen's second cousin (Rufus, who was Ben's father, and J. H., Vernon's grandfather, were brothers), also created talk. Melvin had long operated a pottery that made traditional ware—churns, jugs, and crocks. As times changed, he had focused more on dinnerware and decorative pieces, like J. B. Cole's pottery and Jugtown. Vernon and his siblings had learned to throw at a young age. He had left school before finishing and had been making pottery for his father. Bobby, his 21-year-old brother, went with Vernon to Jugtown.

Vernon, Bobby, and Charles Moore, who lived nearby, kept the pottery open. Juliana died in April 1962, and in less than six months Maré died too—and with him, his plans for the pottery. Howard Broughton, Maré's executor, arranged to keep the pottery open and leased it to Vernon on a month-to-month basis. In 1968, Country Roads, a nonprofit corporation co-founded by folk historian Ralph Rinzler and Nancy Sweezy to foster traditional arts in the U.S., bought Jugtown Pottery. Sweezy, a trained potter, was hired by the corporation to run Jugtown (photo 17).

When Vernon came to Jugtown in 1961, he had faced a familiar situation: What should he make and what should it look like? Vernon was good, though a young and inexperienced potter. He copied traditional Jugtown shapes, but he couldn't be guided by Jacque Busbee's skilled criticism and broad knowledge. Hard feelings remained from the confusion over the competing corporations. Prospective customers were not sure the quality of the wares was being sustained. Business fell off.

In 1968, the intervention of an outside institution or person (now known as "cultural intervention") to preserve traditional crafts was not a new idea. Indeed, the Busbees and Ben Owen had done so when they skillfully appropriated Asian forms to infuse new life into their pottery. And they were not alone. Magazines and tourists had long brought new ideas and changing tastes to Seagrove potters. But Nancy Sweezy's intervention at Jugtown was not an easy one. Vernon said, "It was at a bad time."[4]

And it was a bad time for a variety of reasons. Barely two miles up the road from Jugtown, Ben Owen had opened his shop. Although arthritis began to take its toll on Ben, he continued to make the same work there that he'd created at Jugtown. Owen hired local potters like Farrell Craven and Boyce Yow to throw, while his son, Ben junior, was responsible for glazing and firing. Other potteries—those of Melvin Owens, the Teagues, the Chriscoes, the Aumans, and J. B. Cole—were stiff competition for sales.

Continuing social and cultural changes also made it a challenging time in Seagrove. The tension between past values and present demands was great. North Carolina, traditionally a Democratic state, had been shaken by Brown v. Board of Education; the repercussions of that decision were like a slow, burning fire in many hearts and minds. Some early civil-rights actions took place in 1960 at the Greensboro Kress store. By the late 1960s, the Vietnam War was also emerging as a divisive issue; North Carolina was home to several

PHOTO 17: **Nancy Sweezy at Jugtown.**
PHOTO © SAM SWEEZY

large military bases. The assassinations of John and Robert Kennedy and also of Martin Luther King, Jr., caused rioting and looting in some of the state's cities and towns. Television and newspapers brought news of all this strife to an area that was still somewhat isolated and a traditionally conservative stronghold.

The close-knit community had accepted the Busbees, who it turned out were not so different after all—they had shared many of the same values as the local folks. But when Nancy Sweezy arrived, she really was a stranger from the Northeast who, said Vernon, "brought in outsiders and 'hippy-looking' [sic] people. The community

As Vernon's confidence and experience grew, he became increasingly critical of his own work. He wanted to make his own versions of the Jugtown canon of Asian-influenced forms and the traditional, functional forms that made up the pottery's repertoire.

Country Roads instituted the practice of employing apprentices, many of whom were university-educated young people (photo 18, page 74). These people brought their own ideas, experience, and knowledge, which broadened the pottery's outlook and helped to reshape its wares. Among them were Pamela Lorette, who married Vernon in 1981, and David and Mary Farrell, who opened Westmoore Pottery in 1977.

CONTINUING SOCIAL AND CULTURAL CHANGES ALSO MADE IT A CHALLENGING TIME IN SEAGROVE. THE TENSION BETWEEN PAST VALUES AND PRESENT DEMANDS WAS GREAT.

couldn't deal with it."[5] Sweezy's organization potentially held the key to the survival of Jugtown. So the two of them got to work solving pottery problems: shapes, bodies, glazes.

As Jugtown's newest guiding light, Sweezy saw that there were several issues to be tackled. First, traditional lead glazes were prohibited by the U.S. Food and Drug Administration in 1971, and earthenware colors like white and "true" orange had to be reformulated, though they continued to make frogskin and salt-glazed ware on a regular basis.[6]

Another issue was a technical challenge. Local clay had always been used at Jugtown, but it could be difficult to throw and it sometimes cracked or even exploded in the firing. Although a certain percentage of firing losses had always been an accepted part of the production process, they weren't acceptable to Sweezy the businessperson. She was also an accomplished potter in her own right, and determined to see Country Roads succeed. She and Vernon experimented to change the clay mixture they used. In time, local clay was mixed with clay from other sources, and additional testing determined the best temperature range to fire the glazes. These changes created stronger clay bodies and better outcomes.

Sweezy stayed at Jugtown for 12 years. Her dedication to the craft garnered her acceptance by the community. Locals came to appreciate the efforts of her partnership with Vernon, Bobby (who worked with glazes there), and with the apprentices. Concurrent with this period of increasing awareness of craft as a valuable aspect of American culture and history, Vernon became a nationally recognized potter, and his wife, Pam, became an increasingly important partner—not only as a potter herself but also as an expert in color and glazing. Jugtown emerged from the troubles of the late '60s and early '70s buoyed by the increasing interest in the past and by the contemporary craft movement. Vernon has said that "if the peace movement and the flower child movement hadn't happened, the pottery business would never have been revived. People 35 years old and up had lost interest in pottery at that time. Handmade stuff was out, nobody cared about handcrafted stuff. Then the flower children came along—'back to the earth' and all that, and it was what they wanted. And then it didn't take but a few years of them being interested before their parents got interested."[7]

When Vernon went to work for Country Roads, he continued to make the useful ware of the

Busbee years, which supported rather than competed with the production of the oriental translations. Sweezy reformulated the lead glazes to make them nontoxic, so as to continue the familiar earthenware colors: tobacco spit, bright orange, buff yellow, and opaque white. Jugtown's ware had always been fired in many different kilns, but as the clay and glazes were modified, other kilns had to be added. An oil kiln had been introduced in 1969 (and was eventually replaced by two gas car kilns some 20 years later). Another oil-fired kiln was used for salt glazing, plus four wood-fueled groundhog kilns were used, two of them dating back to the Busbee years.

There were also experiments with cobalt and a copper reduction glaze to develop one comparable to the famous Chinese blue of the past. Photo 19 shows two very different Han vases. Vernon's lighter colored glaze is more like a ceramic skin. The darker one by Ben Owen emphasizes the hard, stonelike quality of his (earlier) Jugtown glaze formulation. Both bellies are bulbous, and

PHOTO 19: *Left:* VERNON OWENS, **Han Vase,** *1986. 12¼ x 9½ inches (31.1 x 24.1 cm). Stoneware; copper glaze; stamped "Jugtown", signed "Vernon Owens." Collection of Gallery of Art & Design, North Carolina State University, Leonidas J. Betts Collection, 1991.22.20. Right:* BEN OWEN, **Han Vase,** *circa 1930s. 7¼ x 8 inches (18.4 x 20.3 cm). Stoneware; Chinese blue glaze; stamped "Jugtown". Collection of Gallery of Art & Design, North Carolina State University, transfer from the North Carolina Museum of Art, 1985.000.000*

their glazes stop short to reveal the foot. Vernon's vase has a longer, thinner neck and the handle placement—more upright on the shoulders—emphasizes the pot's vertical, energetic reach into space. Ben Owen's more concentrated form, with dark reds bleeding through the blue, sounds a deep, quiet tone. The two vases are profoundly different, yet neither definitively bests the other. The low, wide vase (photo 20) by Vernon, with its dark, experimental blue-green glaze, suggests another attempt to achieve the elusive Chinese blue. It emphasizes how important color is in relation to shape.

Jugtown also made salt-glazed utilitarian stoneware that paid homage to that of the 19th century, yet such newer work has an intensely contemporary execution. The jug's increased height emphasizes the sculptural form (photo 21). As with the Han vase, Owens pulled in the shoulder tightly to give the jug an upward, lifting energy that is resolved in the fineness of the neck. Repeating rings at regular intervals on the pot's belly and shoulder add a rhythm that strengthens that energy, and the refined salted surface recalls the tight skin of Himer Fox's jar (see page 28).

Some oriental translations were also salt glazed. Two vases, a white one by Ben Owen and a salt-glazed one by Vernon Owens (photo 22, page 76), show how each maker could give the same form a radically different feeling. Their profiles alone focus attention on the way each potter handled the shoulder and treated the transition from shoulder to flared neck. The shoulder of Vernon's vase is more definitive; its tighter, more muscular tension rises to a flared rim This salted piece has a quickness and confidence in its crisper form. By contrast, the shoulder of Ben's rises and flows smoothly up to the rim. The vase is lyrical and its color reinforces the gentle and peaceful feeling of the form.

Under Pam and Vernon's direction, Jugtown's wares gained a different kind of energy. Compare the two beautiful pairs of candlesticks in photo 23, page 76. The taller salt-glazed stoneware candlestick by Vernon is painfully thin, with a profile that suggests energy, balance, and lightness. Ben's shorter earthenware form has a more substantial body. Its shaft is physically and aesthetically heavier, the foot seems to flow more solidly into the

PHOTO 21:
VERNON OWENS, **Jug,** *1982–1986. Height, 17½ inches (44.5 cm). Stoneware; salt glaze; signed "Vernon Owens", stamped "Jugtown". Collection of Gallery of Art & Design, North Carolina State University, Leonidas Betts Collection, 1991.22.017*

shaft, and the upturned cup is deep and ready for work. Their overall result is one of a quieter and more contained form that asserts its presence with dignity. Vernon's wiry candlestick rises from a broader foot, as if to balance its more radical taper into the candle cup and its surrounding rim. The effect is exuberance and power.

How the Jugtown Pottery evolved is not only illustrated by the differences in how Ben Owen and

PHOTO 20: ATTRIBUTED TO VERNON OWENS, **Vase,** *1984. 4¾ x 6½ inches (12 x 16.5 cm). Stoneware; experimental glaze; stamped "Jugtown". Collection of Gallery of Art & Design, North Carolina State University, Leonidas J. Betts Collection, 1991.22.023*

Vernon Owens approached the same forms but in
how the two potters grew as craftsmen. Ben grew
under the tutelage of the educated, well-traveled,
and sophisticated Busbees and from the influence
of the crafts revival they exposed him to. Vernon
and Bobby Owens benefited from Sweezy's profes-
sional education, expertise, and knowledge of the
importance of the craft market, whether consumer or collector. But these influences were only
part of the picture. Neither Ben nor Vernon
worked in isolation; tradition, family attitudes and
values, their growing experience and confidence,
their relationships with friends, other potters, the
larger world—all helped them shape their pots.

THE OLD ORDER CHANGES

The Seagrove and Jugtown potters changed as
their skills and knowledge grew and evolved but
they were not, as Beth Thompson found out,
alone. The wind blew in the direction of other
Seagrove-area potters, too. In the 1980s, new ones
started working and older potters retired, yet certain patterns repeated themselves. Work was
being made in the Seagrove area that reinforced
the power of tradition even as it demonstrated the
insistence of change.

PRODIGALS

C. B. ("Charlie") Craven was a descendant of
J. D. Craven, and he and his siblings were raised
making pottery. One brother, Farrell, worked for
C. R. Auman, at the Teagues' and Plank Road
potteries. At 18, C. B. left Seagrove to work in the
High Point furniture factories. Between about
1928 and 1942, while working for several different
North Carolina potteries, including North State in
Sanford and Royal Crown in Merry Oaks, C. B.
learned to throw very large pots. The war closed
the Royal Crown pottery, and after 30 years in
the produce business in Raleigh, C. B. retired in
1973, built himself a shed, bought an electric kiln,
and began to work in clay again.

C. B. Craven fired some of his thrown earthenware and stoneware at Teagues' shop (photo 24).
His salt-fired stoneware (photo 25) was fired
at Jugtown, and it stands as a testament to his
mature skill. The churn, painted with a "3,"
displays splashes of cobalt on the shoulder
between lug handles that are so tightly applied
it is almost as if they've been pulled directly out

of the body, like sleeves or shoulder pads under the clay skin. This tight crispness reinforces the powerful sense of the clay body as not only malleable but also strong and compact. The three salt-glazed, wood-fired lidded jars or canisters in the same photo evoke earlier storage jars and jugs, but these are transformed by lids that are almost prissy, with their little finials and even tinier nipples rising from raised circles. The delicate lids are light and charming but almost too small in proportion to the size of the jars themselves; they seem to sink down timidly, as if not too eager to be seen.

These pieces illustrate the ongoing seduction that salt glazing holds for Seagrove potters, and they show clearly the desirable characteristics of ware made at Jugtown. Their orange-peel surfaces are unique and uniformly uneven, attractive to the hand and the eye, with a sense of the vessels' strength and impermeability. The salt's irregular effects recall the unpredictability of the craft's process, just as their gorgeous colors reference the cool springs and soft rain of Seagrove itself. Though it lives in the present, Craven's work calls out to the past. It is classic. He used the potter's language like a poet, creating work in elegant, familiar, unique forms.

Joe Owen, Ben Owen's brother and Melvin's first cousin, was another potter whose work maintained a continuity with the past. Joe had made both wholesale and retail pottery, and in the 1950s, he was part owner of the Glenn Art Pottery Company, a company that made several hundred thousand flower pots a year in the Seagrove area's largest kiln. In 1956, he gave up the large operation and moved to a small workshop near his home, throwing and firing large and small earthenware pieces in an oil-fired kiln until 1981, when fuel costs forced him to replace it with two electric kilns. Over time, Joe's earthenware planters, pitchers, churns, and jars were increasingly made to order for collectors, who revered him for his venerable age as well as his ability (photo 26, page 78). He stayed busy but he viewed present-day culture with trepidation, allowing that he was not pleased with how people were living and working; no one had time to chat or to grow flowers anymore.

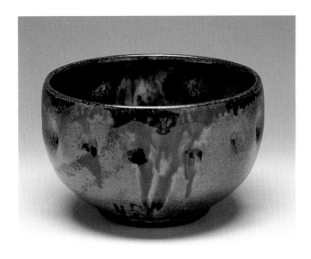

PHOTO 24: C. B. CRAVEN, **Thumbprint Bowl,** *circa 1982–1986. 3½ x 9 inches (8.9 x 22.9 cm). Stoneware; Teague "specky" glaze; stamped "C. B. Craven and Teagues Pottery". Collection of Gallery of Art & Design, North Carolina State University, Leonidas J. Betts Collection, 1991.22.085*

PHOTO 25: C. B. CRAVEN, **Lidded Jar with cobalt decoration (churn) and Set of Three Canisters with Lids,** *circa 1984. Tallest, 15¾ inches (40 cm). Stoneware; salt glaze, cobalt decoration; stamped "C. B. Craven" and "Jugtown". Collection of Gallery of Art & Design, North Carolina State University, Leonidas J. Betts Collection, (left to right) 1991.22.048a&b, 1991.22.010a&b, 1991.22.009a&b, 1991.22.048a&b*

PHOTO 26: JOE OWEN, **Churn,** *1982–1986. Height, 15 inches (38.1 cm). Earthenware; white glaze. Collection of Gallery of Art & Design, North Carolina State University, Leonidas Betts Collection, 1991.22.024a&b*

PHOTO 28: BEN OWEN MASTER POTTER, **Single Table Service,** *circa 1960. Dinner plate: 10⅛ inches (10.6 cm) in diameter; salad plate: 8½ inches (21.6 cm) in diameter; cup: 2¾ x 3¾ inches (7 x 9.5 cm); saucer: 7 inches (17.8 cm) in diameter. Earthenware; clear lead glaze; all pieces stamped "Ben Owen Master Potter". Collection of Gallery of Art & Design, North Carolina State University, gift of Louise and Banks Talley, Jr., (left to right) 2001.004.050, 2001.004.044, 2002.004.0019, 2001.004.038*

In 1986, Joe Owen died without having achieved the level of recognition of some of his relatives. Leonidas Betts, a collector of North Carolina vernacular pottery, described Joe as a potter who was flexible and able to adapt to changing working conditions, yet this shy and unassuming man did exactly what pleased him.

PROSPERITY COMES TO TOWN

In the spring of 1959, Ben Owen senior left Jugtown for his new place on Highway 705, where he built a kiln, a pottery shed, and a sales shop (photo 27). The Old Plank Road Pottery allowed him to continue to build on his well-established reputation; his genius was liberated there. Some collectors were already calling his Jugtown work "old Jugtown," to distinguish it from the new.[8] The pottery Ben made at the new shop was just as desirable, and his earthenware dinnerware sets were sought-after wedding gifts (photo 28). The pottery continued to make the classic "oriental translations," but in fewer numbers. He made salt-glazed wine bottles and Korean bowls, frogskin "thumbprint" bowls, tobacco spit–glazed candlesticks, and the matte-white Dogwood vase, though buyers sometimes had to wait a long time to acquire them. Farrell Craven and the other potters who worked at the Plank Road shop continued the high quality associated with Ben's ware. The work sold so quickly that in the early 1970s the shop often had little or nothing for sale. Ben Wade, his son, was not a potter, but he handled the glazing and firing. The pottery had always used journeymen, and as Ben's arthritis became increasingly crippling, production relied more and more on Farrell Craven. In 1972, Farrell, one of the shop's mainstays, died, and soon after the pottery closed.

Ben Wade farmed and raised cattle, although he did not allow the shop or the kiln to fall into disrepair. Ben Owen III, born in 1968, soon showed an interest in and an aptitude for throwing pottery, and began to occasionally make pots under his grandfather's tutelage (photo 29). Ben Wade and his 14-year-old son reopened the pottery as the Ben Owen Pottery Shop shortly before the family patriarch died. The younger Ben threw the traditional forms and glazed in the familiar colors that had made Jugtown's reputation (photo 30). Through his high school and college years, the young potter gained a youthful reputation as he developed skill, awareness, and vision.

J. B. COLE POTTERY

Having succeeded admirably in the years between 1900 and 1950, the J. B. Cole Pottery continued to grow and innovate, producing large amounts of pottery for sale at their huge, barnlike shop near Seagrove. Waymon and his sister, Nell Cole Graves, along with niece Virginia Shelton, Shelton's son Mitchell, and numerous other employees, never wavered in their devotion to making work expeditiously without sacrificing the unique qualities that popularized their ware. They strived to make affordable and authentic hand-made useful ware (containers that held flowers, plants, food, drink, or umbrellas were popular). At times, shoppers lined up outside the pottery in the early-morning hours before a big sale. The pottery's shelves and tables were well stocked. Waymon Cole's allegiance to earthenware production and his use of labor-saving devices made pieces like an Aladdin teapot and large, robust floor vases (photo 31, page 80) possible.

The floor vase's creamy body contrasts with the burnt brown sugar glaze on a turned-out lip, and the effect strengthens both colors' impact. The vase's body rises, with a restrained taper, to a very modest shoulder that flares then contracts, suggesting that the neck and rim might have been applied separately. They have the delightful appearance of having been stitched on, like a turtleneck. This footless pot, probably thrown in three sections and seamlessly joined later, tucks in at the base, with an effect of gathered energy.

By contrast, a metallic, "pewter"-glazed Aladdin teapot utilizes an entirely different scale (photo 32, page 80). Cole's execution of this archetypical teapot form was inspired, he said, by the Bible. His teapot's form has been so severely flattened, however, that the shoulder becomes a wide shelf and the pot's foot is hidden from view. The pot seems to float, contradicting its very substance. Cole attached the handle seamlessly below the shoulder, yet it rises high above the small body. Opposite that, a short, energetic spout emerges in a pointed profile. The lid, with its flattened finial, is guarded by a lid rim. Such a combination—a squat body and a swooping, rising handle—is a strong sculptural statement that is both exotic and appealing: it is a genie lamp and not a teapot at all. Seen in this way, its possible source—the hanging terra-cotta lamps used throughout the Middle

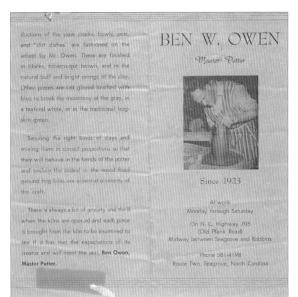

PHOTO 30: BEN OWEN III, **Korean Bowl**, *1983. 4 x 9½ inches (10.2 x 24.1 cm). Stoneware; Chinese blue glaze; signed "Ben Owen III 1983". Collection of Gallery of Art & Design, North Carolina State University, Leonidas J. Betts Collection, 1991.22.099*

PHOTO 31: WAYMON COLE, **Urn**, *1984. 21¼ x 12¼ inches (54 x 31.1 cm). Earthenware; brown-edged cream glaze; signed "WC 1984". Collection of Gallery of Art & Design, North Carolina State University, Leonidas J. Betts Collection, 1991.22.023*

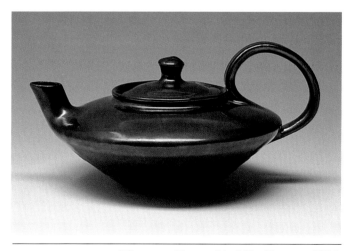

PHOTO 32: WAYMON COLE, **Aladdin Teapot**, *1986. 4½ x 9½ inches (11.4 x 24.1 cm). Earthenware; pewter glaze; signed "WC 86". Collection of Gallery of Art & Design, North Carolina State University, Leonidas J. Betts Collection, 1991.22.053a&b*

East, Greece, and Rome—reveals itself. It is indeed from the Bible, though obviously named for the secular tale.

A larger version from the 1970s (photo 33) has an even more assertive spout, and a potent, reddish version of the burnt brown sugar glaze. This larger pot is a fashion statement, a perfect accompaniment to the era's fashionable palette of avocado green, almond, and brown.

The larger teapot is part of a 40-piece dinner service (photo 34). The plates are particularly impressive because they are so uniform; their rims slant up and away. This warm and inviting dinnerware is very appealing, both modern and traditional.

Though much of the Cole Pottery ware was unsigned, Waymon, Nell, and Virginia Shelton began to sign pieces and sometimes add the date or, as they attained three score and ten years, their ages. Signing was something they had rarely done in the past; doing so signaled a rise in the potters' prestige, as growing numbers of collectors put increasing importance on the pots' provenance. A great deal of their unsigned kitchenware, however, became household staples (photo 35). As fashions changed, the Coles kept pace with a range of glaze colors—dove (a soft gray-brown), lemon yellow, aqua, cobalt blue, burnt brown sugar, red, pewter, and various speckled combinations. Many of their forms remained fixed in the repertoire, although some, like the pitcher shown in photo 36 shows that they absorbed design changes when they wanted to. When J. B. Cole's pottery closed in the 1990s, various family members soon opened their own potteries in the area. Potts Pottery and Shelton's Pottery have retained many of the familiar shapes and colors associated with J. B. Cole's wares.

THE CREEK WIDENS

As time passed, the traditional potteries that had been able to stay in business since 1950 were joined by new makers whose roots were mostly traditional but who also gave their work contemporary personalities. Phil Morgan Pottery, specializing in crystalline ware, and Old Gap Pottery, operated by studio potter Phil Pollett, opened side by side in the late 1970s on Highway 705; their work brought new ideas and forms to the area.

David and Mary Farrell, former apprentices at Jugtown, had left to open Westmoore Pottery in 1977. The Moravian-inspired redware they made was a shock to some of the visitors—and probably to some potters—who were unfamiliar with that pottery tradition.

Milly McCanless's Dover Pottery, which opened in 1983, created some consternation because she made hand-decorated porcelain ware that was outside the range of the Seagrove canon. McCanless had moved to the area in 1972 with her husband, Al, who went to work in Star. In time, Milly learned to make ware at Montgomery Technical College. Dover was Seagrove's fourteenth pottery shop, but Boyd Owens, Melvin's son, remarked that maybe Seagrove had too many shops.

PHOTO 33: ATTRIBUTED TO WAYMON COLE, **Aladdin Teapot,** *circa 1976–1978. 5 x 10 inches (12.7 x 25.4 cm). Earthenware; brown-edged cream glaze. Collection of Gallery of Art & Design, North Carolina State University, gift of Daniel McLawhorn, 1996.017.000*

PHOTO 35: J. B. COLE POTTERY, **Juice Cup and Berry Bowl,** *1982–1986. Cup: 3 x 3¼ inches (7.6 x 8.3 cm); bowl: 1¼ x 4¼ inches (3.2 x 10.8 cm). Earthenware; dove glaze; applied sticker on bowl reads "handcrafted by J. B. Cole Pottery Seagrove, NC". Collection of Gallery of Art & Design, North Carolina State University, Leonidas J. Betts Collection, (cup) 1991.22.032; (bowl) 1991.22.049*

PHOTO 34: J. B. COLE POTTERY, **Salad Plate, Soup Bowl, and Plate,** *circa 1976–1978. Salad plate: 9 inches (22.9 cm) in diameter; soup plate: 4½ inches (11.4 cm) in diameter; bowl: 5 inches (12.7 cm) in diameter. Earthenware; brown-edged cream glaze. Collection of Gallery of Art & Design, North Carolina State University, gift of Daniel McLawhorn, (left to right) 1996.017.059, 1996.017.060, 1996.017.003*

PHOTO 36: VIRGINIA SHELTON, **Pitcher,** *1983. 8 x 7¼ inches (20.3 x 18.4 cm). Earthenware, white glaze; signed "VA 1983" on side. Collection of Gallery of Art & Design, North Carolina State University, Leonidas J. Betts Collection, 1991.22.043*

Billy Ray Hussey fired his first kiln in 1986, after working at Jugtown and for Melvin Owens at his pottery on Busbee Road (photo 37). From the excellent tradition of skills and practices he learned from Melvin and Boyd, Hussey was anything but a classic Seagrove potter. At Melvin's, Hussey had introduced new and more complicated sculptural forms to the repertoire of vases, pitches, bowls, and tableware. He was inspired by Staffordshire dogs, Shenandoah Valley lions, and farmyard chickens (photo 38). Seagrove potters had always made such "whimsies." Charles Moore's chickens and Boyce Yow's famous catfish (photo 39) were long made at Jugtown. But Hussey's work was imbued with energy and a growing confidence that drove his ambition. He encouraged Melvin to make face jugs (photo 40, page 84), a form that had never been associated with traditional Seagrove pottery. Fantastic creatures and inscriptions adorned large jars (photo 41, page 84), and Hussey began to call himself a folk or visionary potter. His figures were sought after, kiln openings were well attended, and the work sold quickly.

About the time that Hussey started his own pottery, he became a partner in another enterprise, the Southern Folk Pottery Collectors Society (SFPCS), an organization that had originated in Connecticut but which quickly found a home near Seagrove. The Society promoted the sale, by absentee auction, of what Hussey and co-founder Roy Thompson identified as Southern folk pottery, with particular emphasis on North Carolina work. Hussey, following in the Aumans' footsteps, turned his considerable energy to the history of the area and its potters. He also learned to identify the work of different hands, and became a qualified appraiser. And while the presence of the SFPCS added a new dimension to Seagrove's stature, it did so to mixed reviews. Now the sale of old ware competed with that of the new. Hussey became a resident expert on the area's ceramics and those of the entire Southern folk pottery tradition. Hussey's success as a maker and an entrepreneur has been tied to increased awareness of the significance of Seagrove's potting tradition and its makers—the same historical consciousness that spurred the

PHOTO 37: *Left:* MELVIN OWENS, **Teapot,** *1982. 8½ inches (21.6 cm) to finial. Right:* NANCY OWENS, **Teapot,** *1982. 5¼ inches (14.6 cm) to finial. Both: stoneware; salt glaze, cobalt decoration. Collection of Gallery of Art & Design, North Carolina State University, (left) 1991.22.079 a & b; (right) Leonidas J. Betts Collection, 1991.22.080a&b*

Aumans to collect and exhibit 19th- and early 20th-century wares. Hussey claims Rinzler as a major inspiration, and in fact Rinzler's collection was the substance of the Society's first important sale.

Still other potters opened their own shops in the 1980s. Hickory Hill was founded by Danny Marley, a functional potter who, inspired by the Farrells and their work, had studied with them. Mark and Meredith Haywood have made ware at their Whynot Pottery, near Erect, since 1982. Robert Armfield, who had apprenticed with the Aumans, opened Oakland Pottery in the early 1980s. And Sid Luck, another returning prodigal, opened his shop in 1987. By the mid 1990s, Seagrove's cadre of potters totaled almost 70. It continued to grow as established potters took on apprentices and Montgomery Community College's pottery program trained local people who wanted to enter the trade. The role of the Seagrove tradition was changing again. While functional wares of all kinds continued to be made, the sources and influences that shaped new work expanded. The world was wide and its creative possibilities unlimited.

PHOTO 38: BILLY RAY HUSSEY, **Crowing Chicken,** *1986, 8 x 7 x 7 inches (20.3 x 17.8 x 17.8 cm). Stoneware; metallic and salt glaze. Collection of Gallery of Art & Design, North Carolina State University, Leonidas J. Betts Collection, 1991.022.100*

PHOTO 39: *Left:* BOYCE YOW, **Catfish,** *circa 1982–86. Length, 9 inches (22.9 cm). Stoneware; Albany slip, salt glaze; inscribed "Boyce Yow, Jugtown NC". Right:* CHARLES MOORE, **Chicken,** *1985. Height, 8½ inches (21.6 cm). Earthenware; lead glaze; signed "Charles Moore". Both: collection of Gallery of Art & Design, North Carolina State University, Leonidas J. Betts Collection, (left) 1991.22.035; (right) 1991.22.038*

THE MOVE TO FINE CRAFT

In 1996, the Mint Museum of Art in Charlotte mounted *Southern Arts and Crafts: 1890–1940*. It was just as important an exhibition for all of North Carolina as the McKissick Museum's 1994 show, *New Ways for Old Jugs*, had been for Jugtown alone. Exhibitions like these embodied the renewed interest in traditional crafts that had flowered 20 and 30 years earlier. Contemporary craft's ascendancy buoyed its practitioners.

Although Seagrove-area potters experienced uneven and unpredictable financial success, by the mid 1990s still more potteries had opened. Old pots that had once been vital to the survival of Seagrove's agricultural economy became essential for other reasons. They became objects to be studied and acquired for their beauty and for their utility as relics and documents of the past. The new work had some of the same kind of appeal and could also put the public in contact with craftspeople whose visions were diverse and engaging.

At the start of a new millennium, the nearly 100 potters in the Seagrove area face new challenges. Put gently, how many potteries can find buyers for their wares? More critically, how many potters will find the confidence, courage, and energy—as well as the vision—to make work that can stand forth, not simply to compete in a market, but to embody a vision that is attractive and inspiring? Historically, Seagrove's traditional wares have been strong because the work has embodied values drawn from a relatively homogenous community where self-reliance, diligence, independence, and integrity are embodied.

The stories of the potters that follow may provide some answers.

PHOTO 40: MELVIN OWENS, **Face Jug**, *1983. 10 x 7 inches (25.4 x 17.8 cm). Earthenware; clear glaze; inscribed "To L.J.B. Melvin Owens 1983". Collection of Gallery of Art & Design, North Carolina State University, Leonidas J. Betts Collection, 1991.22.073*

PHOTO 41: BILLY RAY HUSSEY, **Bank with Seated Figure**, *1986. 13 x 6 inches (33 x 15.2 cm). Earthenware; clear glaze; inscribed "The Longest, Hottest, Driest, Summer", signed "BH" on bottom, "First kiln opening" in pencil on bottom. Collection of Gallery of Art & Design, North Carolina State University, Leonidas J. Betts Collection, 1991.22.125*

BEN OWEN III,
**Dome-Lidded
Cookie/Cracker
Jar.** *12 x 9 inches
(30.5 x 22.9 cm).
Earthenware;
tobacco spit glaze;
signed "Ben Owens
III, 1986."
Collection of Gallery
of Art & Design,
North Carolina
State University,
Leonidas J. Betts
Collection,
1991.22.099 a & b*

NOTES

1 During the 1960s, Representative Bowles engaged the North Carolina Department of Conservation to help promote direct sales of pottery to tourists, and his department helped fund ads for magazines like *National Geographic*.

2 Sweezy, *Raised In Clay*, 245.

3 Some information about this period came from the author's conversations with Ben and Margaret Williams, Raleigh, N.C., in 2004–2005.

4 DeNatale, Douglas, Jane Przybysz, and Jill R. Severn. *New Ways for Old Jugs*, 72.

5 Ibid.

6 The term "frogskin" is thought to have been coined by Jacques Busbee sometime in the 1920s. It was part of the Jugtown glaze repertoire and later that of Ben Owen Pottery.

7 DeNatale, Douglas, Jane Przybysz, and Jill R. Severn. *New Ways for Old Jugs*, 72.

8 So closely associated are Jugtown and Owen that even today I find myself explaining to collectors that work stamped "Jugtown" was made there *but* not necessarily by Ben Owen senior; and that the "Ben Owen Master Potter" stamp was used at Owen's Old Plank Road Pottery.

CHAPTER 4

SEAGROVE TODAY

CAROL GENTITHES, **Chagall Teapot,** *2005*

PRESENT-DAY POTTERIES

PHOTO 1: **Frank Harmon, FAIA, architect, North Carolina Pottery Center, exterior.** PHOTO BY TIM AYERS; COURTESY OF NORTH CAROLINA POTTERY CENTER

PHOTO 2: **North Carolina Pottery Center, interior. Installation on the history of pottery surrounds the central temporary-exhibition space.** PHOTO BY TIM AYERS; COURTESY OF NORTH CAROLINA POTTERY CENTER

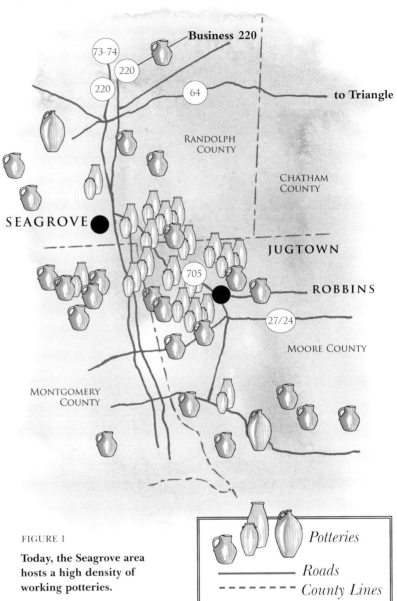

FIGURE 1

Today, the Seagrove area hosts a high density of working potteries.

Traffic is heavy on N.C. Highway 705, the "Pottery Highway" that very nearly follows the route of the Old Plank Road. Today it connects Seagrove to Robbins, about 10 miles down the road. It's a warm spring Saturday and the fields are green, trees are in bud, and signs and banners proclaim the pottery shops open for business. Tourists are encouraged to explore 705 via signs that say "Area Potteries." In town, a few retailers show the work of many potters (plus candles, candy, cards, and the like), though not all of it is local work. But the true heart of Seagrove—individual studios and shops with working potters—is spread out along the smaller roads, waiting to be discovered.

Near the town's retail stores, the North Carolina Pottery Center (photo 1) sits, a modern symbol of Seagrove's heritage. The profile of the red brick building with its standing-seam metal roof recalls the barns of this farming region and the sheds where potters have worked for the past two centuries. Inside the Center, exhibits present North Carolina's pottery history and showcase contemporary work from the Seagrove area and beyond (photo 2).

Also on the Center's premises is a building used for classes and workshops, and a multi-chambered kiln built by a team led by Douglass Rankin and Will Ruggles, master potters from Roan Mountain in the western part of the state (photo 3, page 88).

PHOTO 3: **The NCPC Education Building, which has a stepped kiln, and hosts school groups, special events, and pottery workshops.**

PHOTO 4: CAROL GENTITHES, **Teapot with Bee,** *2004. 8 x 9 x 4½ inches (20.3 x 22.9 x 11.4 cm). Porcelain; various glazes*

This kiln emphasizes that the Center itself is an active environment for potters. Close by is the Museum of Traditional Pottery, which celebrates the local makers and their work. While the shops, Center, and Museum can guide visitors to the remarkable diversity and variety of work to be found within a mere 15-mile radius, they are also symbols of the transformations that have shaped the lives of the potters. Many visitors return repeatedly, drawn by the opportunity to buy wares directly from a maker who is willing to share something of his or her personality or of the history of the place. (Occasionally, it seems these intangibles are embodied in the work itself.)

Seagrove's present-day economy is based on tourism. Its prosperity also relies on its physical assets (clay, and wood for firing) and on the remarkable resources of the community of knowledgeable people—now academically trained ones as well as those who have grown up in local potting families. Significantly, the state of North Carolina has itself discovered the importance of its pottery history. Seagrove, with its 200-year legacy, has helped lead the way. Such an abundance of ceramic production is only found in a few other locales in the world, places such as Shigaraki in Japan, and La Borne, France. Seagrove plays host to many potters whose wares are enormously varied yet whose futures seem no more assured, in some ways, than those of the potters who lived there in 1900.

PRESENT-DAY SEAGROVE

North Carolina is now the eleventh most populous state in the nation. Roughly 3 million people live within about two hours' drive of Seagrove, and newer, wider highways have made the area more accessible than ever before. The busy cities of Charlotte and the Research Triangle of Raleigh, Durham, and Chapel Hill have growing urban populations; the latter also supports three major universities. These urban areas, plus the cities of the Triad (Greensboro, High Point, and Winston-Salem), make up three of Seagrove potters' major markets. Today, no potter is truly isolated; those whose shops range along Highway 705 may have the marginal advantage of easy access, but a proliferation of signage and information makes it possible to visit every shop in the area.

Nevertheless, prosperity in rural areas can be fleeting. Many small towns in North Carolina, once bustling textile and furniture centers, have nearly died since the big industries left. Similarly, Seagrove potters find themselves, as always, vulnerable to forces they cannot control any more than the textile workers could prevent outsourcing. For now, there is a huge amount and variety of pottery to be had.

In Seagrove, it's possible to acquire almost anything that can be made of clay. Tableware and kitchen supplies are available in every imaginable color, from shiny lavender, purple, red, and orange to soft yellow, peach, pinks, and blue mattes. Black, whether matte or shiny, seems to be making a strong comeback just now.

You can find perfectly painted plates, stretched and pulled platters and bowls, containers that look as if they were inspired by Jackson Pollock paintings, and miniatures of everything: batter bowls and pitchers, tea sets and cups, mugs and vases True to form, potters have even devised new interpretations of old forms, such as the popular coffee cup–handled colander, first devised at Magnolia Pottery, that can drain a single can of vegetables or fruit. You can commission a tile wall, a sink, patio, bench, or an inlaid-tile table of any size. A dinnerware service might match your wallpaper, or coordinate with candles and linens. Several potters now make dinnerware decorated with eagles, the American flag, and other patriotic symbols.

Clay creatures are available in many sizes, from miniatures to garden size. Once considered mere whimsies, usually pinched from leftover clay, these objects are sometimes very much sought after. The Jugtown Pottery has always been a source of ceramic animals; for collectors, some of the most popular are the catfish that were made by Boyce Yow, but cats, elephants, chickens, and pigs have all been part of the repertories of many if not most of the Seagrove potteries. J. B. Cole's pottery made both recognizable animals and miniature beasts, which Nell Cole Graves sometimes called "dinoshores."

Carol Gentithes at the Johnston and Gentithes Art Pottery combines elements drawn from useful ware with ideas and images drawn from popular culture and contemporary artists (photo 4). Billy Ray Hussey fashioned Staffordshire dogs, Bell lions (named for the lions made by the Bell pot-

PHOTO 5: **Billy Ray Hussey**

tery in Virginia), and exuberant chickens when he worked at Melvin Owens's pottery (photo 5). Since he opened his own pottery in 1986, his sculptural repertoire has expanded: children riding on pigs, bears with honey pots, goats, potters at the wheel, and face jugs. Hussey describes himself as a visionary folk potter and considers himself aligned with untrained as well as traditional folk artists whose inspirations may include religion and spirituality and whose work derives from a need to express a very personal vision. Interest in this kind of work began in the last quarter of the 20th century.

Commercial glazes and prepared clays have expanded the potter's range of work. Seasonal decorations—angels, Santa Clauses, snowmen, and pumpkins—are very much a part of some

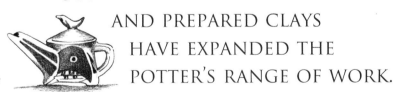

COMMERCIAL GLAZES AND PREPARED CLAYS HAVE EXPANDED THE POTTER'S RANGE OF WORK.

shops' inventories. Crystal King at Crystal King's Pottery, for example, models figures and modest Biblical tableaux. It seems only appropriate that figurative pieces, made of clay for millennia, should once more be a part of ceramic production in the Seagrove area.

But, sheer quantity aside, what is the quality of the work? With so much being made by so many

PHOTO 6: DAVID STUEMPFLE, **Vessel,** *2004. 15⅛ x 12¾ inches (38.4 x 32.4 cm). Stoneware; salt glaze*

PHOTO 7: **Westmoore Pottery**

different potters, one cannot help but wonder about its physical quality. That answer is easy. Predictably, the work is technically strong, well and thoughtfully made. It is the underpinning of the place. Then there is its aesthetic quality: is it well designed and sound? That question is more challenging to answer.

Each maker has his or her independence, a particular and personal vision. Each visitor who discovers Seagrove pottery will also discover this truth. Some only want to make one-of-a-kind pieces that are, for all intents and purposes, works of art. Others find their joy in making the utilitarian wares that have always fed the potter and his family. Some potters combine their interests, making useful ware as well as work that is for domestic adornment and decoration. A fair way to evaluate the aesthetics of the area should take into account the goals that drive the maker. Seagrove offers each visitor the opportunity to meet many makers and to discover work that satisfies a variety of their personal needs. This aesthetic abundance is an amazing gift (photo 6).

SHOPS AND STORES

Retail pottery businesses in Seagrove are no longer seasonal; in fact, many potters feel a heightened sense of responsibility to accommodate the public. Their hours, for example, have bowed to this reality, although few are open on Sunday. Perhaps just as much as the wares, their shops are essential marketing and sales tools. Potters first sold their wares from their sheds and yards, from the beds of wagons, and in hardware stores. Then they added catalogs and shipped to buyers in other places. The Westmoore potters built a red-brick shop when they established their business in 1977. The owners, however, were warned that no one would stop there because tourists expected the traditional shed or log cabin (photo 7). The Farrells proved the naysayers wrong.

The names of Seagrove's pottery shops sometimes have appealing associative qualities. Old House Pottery, Rock House Pottery, Turn and Burn, Old Hard Times, Pot Luck, Jugtown, From the Ground Up, and Down to Earth are all names that evoke homey sincerity and authenticity. Others, such as the Lantern Hill, Cagle Road, and Whynot potteries, use more pragmatic location names. Still others employ the potters' own names, as do Ben Owen Pottery, Cady Clay Works, Avery Pottery and Tileworks, and Luck's Wares.

Some shops are located in private homes, with a public area that might be fitted with track lights, elegant shelving, area rugs, and smart paint colors to complement the goods for sale. Retail items such as candles, table linens, or garden-related supplies augment the offerings of dinnerware and planters. Occasionally the potter lives in a private section of the house; the potting shed, with all its attendant messiness, may be screened from public view.

Another kind of store (whether called a gallery or a shop) utilizes a freestanding building or an addition close by the potter's home or workshop. The mother of all retail-space pottery shops may well be the rustic log cabin that Juliana Busbee created at Jugtown Pottery in the 1920s (photo 8). It epitomized her allegiance to an idealized Colonial American

PHOTO 8: **Jugtown Pottery Sales Shop, circa 1963**

PHOTO 9: **Jugtown Pottery Sales Shop, circa 2000.** COURTESY OF JUGTOWN POTTERY

PHOTO 10: **Dirt Works Pottery gallery**

PHOTO 11: **Ben Owen Pottery gallery**

PHOTO 12: **Ben Owen Pottery, kiln shed. "Papagama" kiln, far right rear, is original groundhog kiln with additions.**

past and to the Anglo-Saxon potters who valued their independence, and it was these artists whose craft and persistence she and Jacques wanted to preserve and promote. That shop still stands, flanked by a museum, with sensitive additions that have enabled the Owens family to present their wares graciously. Wooden kitchen wares and toys, and candles made to fit Jugtown candlesticks, are also available (photo 9, page 91). Jewelry made from clay and embellished with stones is made by Jennie Lorette, Pam Owens' sister.

The Dirt Works Pottery exemplifies a more contemporary shop style; its long rectangular space and high, floor-to-ceiling windows are reminiscent of an urban art space (photo 10); the pots themselves are arranged as if for exhibition. Other potters have emulated the Dirt Works model. Perhaps the most impressive of these is the Ben Owen Pottery. A modern gallery (photo 11) with shining floors, abundant light, and spare, multi-level display fixtures was added to his grandfather's Old Plank Road shop. An adjacent room is a museum of early Jugtown wares by Ben senior, as well as examples of pottery from other cultures, in glass cases with wall text and labels. This room links the gallery to the dirt-floored, log-built shop where, post-Jugtown, Ben senior once threw and sold pottery. Now it honors the senior Owen's life's work, Jugtown, and the Old Plank Road Pottery. The present workshop is a pristine and spacious pottery studio behind the gallery, and when Owen has special sales he may be at work on one of the several wheels just inside the studio door. The studio is pierced with many large windows, through which visitors can see Ben at the wheel even before they enter the spacious workshop; beyond the throwing room, connecting rooms and spaces efficiently organize the entire pottery process. Beside the studio is an enormous shed that houses several kilns, including his grandfather's much-modified groundhog kiln, which Ben still uses today (photo 12).

Another kind of shop is Sid Luck's Ware, off Adams Road (photo 13). The shop is a long, one-story shed that contains his stock for sale, the working spaces, kilns, and a sort of office. At the open, back end of the shop stands a large wood-fired kiln. The majority of Luck's work is traditional vernacular wares, sometimes salt glazed. In addition, Luck has started to make the very popular face jug. His two sons are also potters, though Jason plans to practice law (just as his father taught school for many years) before returning to the area to become a potter. Matt Luck is a chicken farmer; his long, low houses can be seen from the back of Luck's shop. This enterprise is another way he can be sure he can provide for his family while he is a potter. Luck's shop is neither particularly neat nor artistically arranged; it says, "this is about making pottery." Other direct and utilitarian potters' shops reflect such philosophies too (photo 14).

In addition to making tough decisions about the name or the appearance of the shop and sales area, there is the challenge of staffing. Sometimes the potter, doing double duty, must have a working space in the shop itself, like Sid Luck's or as David and Mary Farrell have done at Westmoore Pottery. Occasionally a bell on the shop door brings the potter from the studio; some post a sign instructing the customer to call the potter to the sales shop with a bell or buzzer. Still others have part-time personnel who may act as bookkeeper or assist with packing and shipping.

Perhaps the biggest responsibility of a potter-retailer, however, is to the demands of production. The shops must be stocked at all times; visitors should not see empty shelves or low stock, which might be interpreted as signs of a failing enterprise, or simply disappoints a potential buyer. Potters who advertise special kiln openings, on their websites or by mail, have found themselves faced with crowds and shelves suddenly bare. These potters have learned to hold back work so their shelves can be restocked even during the heat of a kiln-opening sale. Potters have also learned not to advertise the specific contents of a kiln firing, such as one filled with Chinese Blue or red or wood-fired wares. Pots are thrown, fired, and stocked, without fanfare, while the website and mailings continue to remind the public that the potters are at home. Special orders, the customer understands, can only approximate the ware he sees on the shelves, since firings vary and the results are never identical.

Being responsive to the public can have positive outcomes. Fred Beane, the oldest living potter in

PHOTO 13: **Sid Luck, Luck's Ware. Shop exterior**

PHOTO 14: **Sid Luck, Luck's Ware. Shop interior**

PHOTO 15:
**Fred Beane,
Old House Pottery**

the area (photo 15), produces functional earthen-ware for the table and the kitchen at his Old House Pottery. At one time, Beane's ceramic corn-bread baker (photo 16) incorporated a continuous rim, until one of his users pointed out that the baker was also excellent for making meatloaf and would be even better if a spout was added to pour off accumulated grease. He obliged, adding opposing spouts for even greater convenience. He also created a pierced bean dipper, and learned to make pie birds that look almost exactly like East Anglian examples that are made by potters along the River Stour in England.

Potters say that current fashions influence what the visitor will buy; for example, color trends in home furnishings affect their choice of colors for dinnerware. The desire for the collectible, the unique pieces, is also important, and the wise consumer quickly learns that finding a piece identical to one on the website or in the Pottery Center is unlikely, but equally wonderful work will be available (photo 17). Even Fred Beane's blue and brown cornbread bakers aren't identical, but Beane is a production potter while Samantha Henneke at Bulldog Pottery is not. Her flowerlike,

POTTERY WEBSITES ARE AN INNOVATION THAT REACHES EVEN MORE CUSTOMERS THAN DO THE SHOPS THEMSELVES.

PHOTO 16: FRED BEANE, **Meatloaf and Corn Bread Pan,** *1990. 2½ x 8½ x 2¼ inches (6.4 x 21.6 x 5.7 cm). Stoneware; electric fired to cone 6*

lobed, thin-walled serving bowl with a pale green exterior and a salmon interior can appear in a similar, organic, flowerlike shape but totally different guise based on the effect of a different firing or on her decision to marginally modify the glaze (photo 18).

Pottery websites are an innovation that reaches even more customers than do the shops themselves. Potters also make use of the marketing power of the Seagrove Area Potters Association, which advertises special events and lists each pottery with a brief description of their work (for more information, see 90 Potters, 15 Miles: A Snapshot on page 124). A site that serves the same community is provided by the Museum of

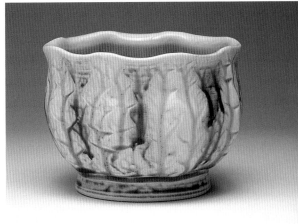

PHOTO 18: SAMANTHA HENNEKE,
Vegetable Bowl, *2003. 4½ x 6¾ inches
(11.4 x 17.1 cm). Porcelain; thrown;
rivulet glaze; oxidation fired*

PHOTO 17: FRED JOHNSTON,
Frogskin Bumby Jar,
*2005.13¼ x 14½ inches
(33.7 x 36.8 cm).
Wood-fired stoneware.*
COURTESY OF ARTIST

Traditional Pottery. Both are linked to county and regional tourism sites, as well as to the North Carolina Arts Council's Craft Trails site. Most potters, like the Ben Owen Pottery and Jugtown, for example, use their sites to announce kiln openings, the range of stock available, and other information of interest. Sites can also include historical details about the pottery, information about the potters, and about how to obtain wares from other locations. Bulldog Pottery uses their site not only to show their wares but also to emphasize the constantly changing and experimental nature of their inventory.

Some potters, however, sell much of their work by advertising through a mailing list, by word of mouth, and through website announcements of three or four kiln openings a year. David Stuempfle and Daniel Johnston are two potters who do not maintain open shops. Their large, single-chambered, wood-fired kilns are derived from the traditional groundhog kiln and larger kiln designs in Thailand and other Asian sites. The size enables the potters to make very large sculptural pieces (as well as many other sizes), and it takes 8 to 12 weeks for the potter to prepare enough pots to fill these monster kilns to capacity. Because of the amount of labor and fuel needed, the kilns must be fired at full capacity, and this happens less often than for smaller kilns (photo 19, page 96).

On the morning of a kiln-opening sale—usually a Saturday—people arrive early. Standing and waiting on a sunny cold Saturday morning in winter, a steamy summer one, or best of all, a warm April morning, creates an immediate community. The crowd gathers; they have come to support the potter, for the satisfaction of acquiring a one-of-a-kind piece, or just to look. Whatever their reasons, these openings create a pervasive sense of the continuity with traditions of the past, and that makes such an event a moving experience.

PHOTO 19: **David Stuempfle's wood-fired kiln, view from the front of kiln to chimney at rear**

PHOTO 20: **Linda Dixon and Drew Krouse**

The Persistence of the Past: Clay, Firing, Production

The persistence of the past takes many forms in the Seagrove area. The potters are willing to use new information about clay, glazes, and kilns, and yet, when it suits their needs, they continue to use old ways of working.

Until the 20th century, pottery making in Seagrove was completely dependent on locally available earthen materials plus the potter's own physical strength and tenacity. Modernization made it possible to prepare clay more easily, first with electric machinery then by simply purchasing prepared clay. The advent of oil, gas, and electric kilns and other such conveniences have been as radically transformative as the invention of premixed tube color was for painters. For most potters, certain time- and labor-intensive steps have disappeared entirely from the process.

Today, the majority of area potters use only commercially prepared clays, although some of them have developed a suitable material from a combination of local and prepared clays. And although it's not as powerful a reason as it once was, some potters remain in the area because of these local clays. Similarly, potters have the option to buy pre-mixed glazes and slips or to obtain the chemicals to devise their own. But no matter which materials they prefer, each has a purely individual and personal approach to both color and clay.

Local clay is a huge attraction for some potters. Linda Dixon was born in Florida and Drew Krouse in New York (photo 20). Krouse's family business is Boston Valley Terra Cotta, which makes architectural terra cotta (floors, roof tiles, chimney pots, fountains, wall tiles, and the like), including large public commissions, such as a mural that

PHOTO 22: LINDA DIXON AND DREW KROUSE, **Vase,** *circa 2005. 21¾ x 11 inches (55.2 x 27.9 cm). Stoneware; various glazes*

PHOTO 24: **LDDK Studio's wood-fired kiln with blue terra-cotta cladding**

PHOTO 25: DAVID STUEMPFLE, **Whiplashed Vessel,** *2005. 22¼ x 10 inches (56.5 x 25.4 cm). Stoneware; wood fired*

PHOTO 26: **Jugtown Pottery, wood-fired kiln**

memorialized the demolished Pennsylvania Station in New York City. The husband-and-wife team were searching for a location where they could execute that commission's tiles in an outdoor setting. In 1991, they came to the Seagrove area and rented the spacious old Glenn Art Studio (a former pottery that specialized in garden ware) for five months. In the process, they learned more about the area—especially the clays (photo 21, page 96).

Their business, LDDK Studios, specializes in small architectural and public art commissions, and uses clay from their land to also make dinnerware, tiles, and decorative pieces (photos 22 and 23, page 97). They built a wood-fired kiln and clad it with bright-blue terra-cotta tiles (photo 24, page 97). Linda and Drew have recently built more kilns in Star, a small town near Seagrove, so they can undertake even larger projects. Their need for space brought them, and the clay has kept them.

Dixon and Krouse share space with some potters who were born into the clay community. All are aware that neither experience nor education can insure financial or ceramic success. Ben Owen III is one of the earliest and best examples of the modern, hybrid-type potter: he was born into a potting family but was formally educated at Pfieffer College and East Carolina University. Owen has traveled in Asia, Europe, and around America studying other traditions to become a potter with his own language. But a potter born into the Seagrove potting community need not study in a four-year studio program or wander for years. Many potters, including Milly McCanless, who, with her pharmacist husband, founded Dover Pottery in 1983, have studied at Montgomery Community College, which offers a ceramics program.

Other local educational opportunities are the annual pottery conference supported by the Randolph County Arts Council, plus workshops and lectures that are presented at the Pottery Center. *Ceramics Monthly* and other craft magazines have long provided advice and guidance to area potters. Courses taught at East Carolina University and other area colleges offer another, different level of training, as do the apprenticeships that some potters have established as a means not only to produce sufficient wares for the market but to help train a new generation of potters.

The freedom to pursue practices like wood firing and salt glazing have attracted still others to the area. Some Seagrove potters (Ben Owen, and Vernon and Pam Owens, among others) have never stopped wood firing, even though it is a notoriously intense undertaking. David Stuempfle, who apprenticed at Jugtown in order to learn how to wood fire, has stayed because he found he couldn't do it anywhere else quite as successfully (photo 25). Now, since the mid-1990s' resurgence of interest in wood-fired, single- and multi-chambered kilns, many more potters have built their own (or share with others). The capriciousness and risk of this method is worth the effort for the color and surface effects that these kilns can produce. The multifaceted experience of longtime practitioners is a hard-won and precious commodity in Seagrove's small but growing circle of wood firers (photo 26).

Experience with clays and glazes builds confidence, and that is something all potters require. The ceramic process is exquisitely sensitive to the chemical makeup of organic clay and glaze materials, and to variations in the fuel, temperature, or atmosphere (i.e., how much oxygen is present) of the firing. Change any one of these and the potter must learn anew. Sometimes another potter offers a very pragmatic solution for a problem, though occasionally only published technical expertise can help. Still, the presence of so much experience is sustaining for everyone.

THE JOURNEY FROM PRODUCTION TO EXPRESSION

The deep well of experience accumulated by the potting families and their kin is part of Seagrove's attraction. Vernon Owens and his brothers, Bobby and Boyd, learned to throw from their father, Melvin. Ben Owen III, a cousin to Melvin's family, learned to throw from his grandfather. The Cole family's potting legacy continues too, in the work of Jenny Potts (Virginia Shelton's granddaughter) and Mitchell Shelton and his family, who were also taught by parents and grandparents. Fred Beane left production potting with C. C. Cole to work for

PHOTO 27:
DANIEL JOHNSTON,
Vase with Medallions,
*2004. 10½ x 7½ inches
(26.7 x 19 cm). Stoneware;
salt and alkaline glaze*

Burlington Industries, but, like others before him, returned to pottery making when he retired.

Whether taught by a father or a familiar, many potters have learned to make pottery through some type of production apprenticeship, and that local tradition persists as well. The production

PHOTO 28: **Chad Brown**

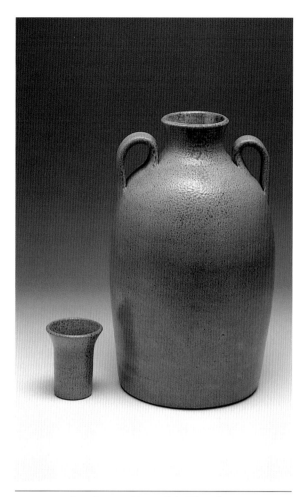

PHOTO 29: SID LUCK, **Jug with Fitted Water Cup,**
*2005. Cup: 4 x 3 ¾ inches (10.2 x 9.5 cm); jug: 14 ¾ x
10 ¾ inches (37.5 x 27.3 cm). Stoneware; salt glaze*

potter is typically young, able, and willing to fit
himself to a demanding system in which speed
and proficiency are highly valued. Through
grueling work, a production potter becomes a
wonderfully proficient one.

Daniel Johnston made production pottery at the
Cole Pottery in the early 1990s. Nell Cole Graves
herself taught him to throw. Production was
Johnston's way to avoid having to work the family
farm yet remain close to the land itself. By the
end of his four-year term at the Coles, Johnston
had become a journeyman. Focusing only on the
wheel itself, he was throwing some 30,000 pieces a
year. During his apprenticeship, Johnston made
time to help other potters build and fire their
kilns and thus learned the differences that kilns
could make in the fired results.

Johnston job-shopped, working for various potters
during different seasons. He was exposed to a

wide variety of designs, styles, types of work,
glazes, kilns, and even marketing strategies. The
young man spent another four years as an apprentice at the Mark Hewitt Pottery near Pittsboro.
Though he was paid less than for production
work, Hewitt's role as mentor allowed Johnston to
focus more on the work's aesthetic and expressive
qualities (photo 27, page 99). Still, there were
times when he also worked as a Seagrove-area production potter; between Hewitt and production,
Johnston put in many seven-day workweeks. At
some point in his development, he came to understand that making pottery was an avenue for personal expression. Johnston's transformation from a
reliable, speedy production potter into a self-critical
and self-conscious maker, whose goals for his work
are still unfolding, is unlike academic training of
any kind.

Chad Brown, the grandson of Graham Chrisco (a
member of another local potting family), is also a
self-described production potter who, after gradu-
ating with a degree in engineering from North
Carolina State University, returned home to make
pottery (photo 28, page 99). Brown works for four
or five different potters during the year, five days
out of the week in the winter and seven days in
the fall, spring, and summer. He is paid $1.25 per
pound of clay thrown and flat fees for more complex pieces. Brown already has a shop and has
built his own kiln; his aspirations are similar
to Daniel Johnston's: to become self sufficient
and independent enough to make work that is
uniquely his own.

The lives of Johnston and Brown, both still in
their 20s, have taken different routes to find
themselves in pursuit of the same goal. They
exude a confidence that is already well tempered
by the hard daily work of throwing ware.

Eck and Will McCanless learned to throw from
their mother, Milly, at the Dover Pottery. After
some time away from Seagrove, they have
returned to make pottery. Each has his own workshop and both will show their work in the Dover
showrooms. Travis Owens, Vernon and Pam's son,
is currently a university design student. He has
made pottery since he was a child and is committed to returning to Jugtown to take up the family
business. On the other hand, Mary and David
Farrell, of Westmoore Pottery, are fairly sure nei-

ther of their children will ever make pottery. The modern reality is that being a member of a potting family no longer determines one's future. Necessity, which drove the choices of earlier makers like the Coles and the Aumans, has given way to different purposes and philosophies of making. Diverse educational opportunities and many experiences, layered onto traditional practices, challenge all Seagrove potters and influence their choices about what to make and how it will look.

THE AESTHETICS OF ABUNDANCE

Nineteenth-century Seagrove-area pottery possesses strong familial resemblances to each other. Puritanical in its simplicity and directness, it still asserts its original purpose with lean or fulsome vigor. The cool colors and nearly oily texture of some of the salt glazing seems particularly appropriate for food preservation in a hot, humid climate; the pots' darkened flashes or uneven coloration seem almost sunburned. Simply put, such ware is characterized by an unselfconscious aesthetic that was created out of the conditions of its production.

Today, potters choose among different formal and stylistic ideas to purposefully create their own self-conscious aesthetic. They may take inspiration from traditional 19th century useful ware, from Asian models, European antecedents, or local work made at any time during the past century. Potters can also employ varied approaches to the way in which they run their businesses. Just as Jugtown's production values under the Busbees were different from those of J. B. Cole's Pottery, similar conditions prevail today. Each potter must decide how much work to make and when to make it, and currently the only clear prevailing trend gives the consumer many choices (photo 29). It is hard to believe the range of work produced and the significant differences in styles, colors, shapes, and decorations. It is hard not to ask, But what is the best work? A still more revealing question is, Why do I want to buy this pottery?

It is a testimony to the vitality of the area that different aesthetic visions have multiplied there. Yet the contrast between the abundance of fine useful and decorative wares for the home and garden and a limited inventory of one-of-a-kind pottery illustrates the differences in the vision, aesthetic,

PHOTO 30: BEN OWEN III, **Two-Handled Vase,** *2005. 12¼ x 6¼ inches (31.1 x 15.9 cm). Stoneware; Chinese blue glaze. Courtesy of artist*

and artistic and personal goals of their makers (photo 30). Most of the potters who make work priced to sell to a broad range of buyers can do so only by means of the convenience and cost effectiveness of using prepared clays, premixed glazes, and electric or gas kiln firing. Those who use locally dug clay, prepare it in a traditional manner, and fire it in wood kilns do so because that process also meets their needs. The fact that some potters do plenty of both means that each approach is not exclusive. But the differences between the two pose questions that can be best answered by the ceramics themselves.

PERSONAL VISIONS

There is a small cadre of potters who have taken their work to the highest level of artistic expression. Their roots vary, having sprung from both generational potters and university- and apprentice-trained studio artists. These contemporary men and women express their deepest commitment to clay as they pay homage to Seagrove's earliest practitioners.

David Stuempfle

David Stuempfle (photo 31) is a delightfully taciturn and intense man. He desires to create work that expresses universal values and gathers traditions from many places. A conversation also reveals his patience and his eagerness to take risks, which are sometimes contradictory forces.

He is committed to wood firing because of its great possibilities. His early work of salt-glazed traditional and gourd-shaped bottles (photo 32), vases, and other containers were generously scaled although not particularly domestic in feeling, but rather like small pieces of sculpture meant to enhance a person's room. The work took advantage of his huge single-chamber wood kiln, which he fired about three times a year. After traveling to Japan, he began to make larger and larger pieces, both coil built and wheel thrown (photo 33). They seem almost human as they stand under the kiln shed or in his yard, dressed in the subdued hues that resulted from their extended exposure to ash and flame in their firings. Their ovoid bodies, animated by handles, necks, and openings, have strong shoulders that taper elegantly to modest bases (photo 34), defying the practical necessity of scaling the base size to overall height. A deformed few, stacked on each other in the kiln, show how Stuempfle has exploited the power of the kiln's intense heat.

PHOTO 31: **David Stuempfle**

PHOTO 32: DAVID STUEMPFLE, **Bottles,** *2002. Tallest, 18 inches (45.7 cm). Stoneware, salt glazed, wood fired*

PHOTO 33: **David Stuempfle Pottery.**
PHOTO BY S. TOURTILOTT

Their colors defy description. Within the range of a gray, green, or brown earthiness, their variations are minute and elaborate. The clay surfaces seem to say that they will be strong enough to withstand centuries, millennia. Salt-glazed gourd vases and bottles (photo 35) appear to be drawn from long ago but they are at every moment also intensely present.

Stuempfle has recently eschewed even introducing salt during the firing. He simply permits wood ash and the fire itself to enhance the work with a variety of textures, color graduations, and shimmering ash runs that delight the eye. His pieces are as individual as people, reinforcing the obvious: that every handmade pot is different from every other, and therein lies their powerful beauty and their purpose (photo 36).

PHOTO 34: DAVID STUEMPFLE, **Jar,** *2005.*
15½ x 13¼ inches
(39.4 x 35 cm).
Stoneware; wood fired

PHOTO 35: DAVID STUEMPFLE, **Cylindrical Vases,** *2005. Each, 12 x 4 inches (30.5 x 10.2 cm). Stoneware; wood fired*

PHOTO 36: DAVID STUEMPFLE, **Vase,** *2005. 19¼ x 9¾ inches (48.3 x 24.8 cm). Stoneware; wood fired*

Ben Owen III

Ben Owen III (photo 37) is a gracious and easy potter to talk with. He is keenly aware of his family's past and of his grandfather's role in reshaping the history of clay in Seagrove. He is also very aware of contemporary craft and the ways it has affected his practice. Self-contained and deeply reflective about pottery and Seagrove's potting community, Owen, like the other potters discussed here, is totally driven to make important, beautiful, and wonderful work. Such energy as his is contained within a framework that is almost musical—measured and rhythmic, always embodied in his forms—changing from major to minor and back again by means of subtle relations of scale and color (photo 38).

Owen too makes very large pieces, some of which are wood fired. The egg vase form created by his grandfather at Jugtown is the source for his Chinese-red Egg Vase (photo 39), whose dimensions far exceed any made before. Its intense, highly reflective red surface very nearly denies the physical exigencies of the material: the piece could be porcelain, plastic, or glass; it could be paper thin or thick walled. Yet the stoneware clay is scaled precisely to carry its own weight. Curiously, the vase has some of the qualities of a Claus

PHOTO 37: **Ben Owen III, Ben Owen Pottery**

PHOTO 39: BEN OWEN III, **Egg Vase**, *2000. 28 x 15 inches (71.1 x 38.1 cm). Earthenware; red glaze. Collection of Gallery of Art & Design, North Carolina State University, gift of Louise Talley and family in honor of Banks Talley's birthday, 2000.000.000*

PHOTO 40: BEN OWEN III, **Equator Vase**, *2004. 24 x 16 inches (61 x 40.6 cm). Stoneware; "copper penny" glaze; wood fired. Collection of Gallery of Art & Design, North Carolina State University, gift of the artist and Lori Ann Owen. T2004.001.001*

Oldenburg outsize sculpture, and with it Owen masterfully exemplifies certain ideas not only about art but also art's relationship to popular culture and materialism. But this is not the only type of work he makes.

A newer vessel is at a far remove from the egg vase (photo 40). Its shape, derived from Asian and European sources, speaks in a language that is both intensely poetic and sculptural. Its simple form (which is nonetheless difficult to make) is adorned with a complex veil of color that changes from bottom to top; golden glitter and striations articulate the entire form and give it the quiet

grandeur of a ritual vessel. Owen's glaze experiments have created rich surfaces that recall hard stones like quartz or Derbyshire fluorspar ("Blue John"). He's inspired by natural shapes from the garden: melons, or ovoid shapes like huge pears, apples, or pumpkins. These forms create links with the natural world as Owen substitutes time-defying clay for the organic, which will, in time, decay; death is replaced with life.

PHOTO 41: **Daniel Johnston,
Daniel Johnston Pottery**

Daniel Johnston

Daniel Johnston is an intense young man (photo 41), critical of his own abilities and others', of his experiences and his circumstances. For him, making pottery is personal expression. This self-sufficient potter has built everything he needs: a large single-chamber wood kiln, fired a few times annually; his shop; even his water cistern, inspired by a trip to Thailand. As an apprentice, Daniel Johnston watched Mark Hewitt create very large pieces, and the synthesis of Johnston's entire experience is becoming evident in his impressive and promising command of clay. His large pieces are derived from a synthesis of Asian and traditional forms. He decorates his wares with stripes,

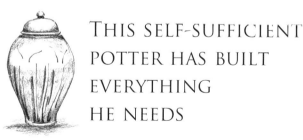

THIS SELF-SUFFICIENT POTTER HAS BUILT EVERYTHING HE NEEDS

swirls, and curves, all gestures that invigorate the surfaces and emphasize the shape of the pot (photo 42).

True to his production roots, Johnston also makes functional ware such as vases, mugs, and bowls. His plates are frequently decorated as if he cannot

PHOTO 42: DANIEL JOHNSTON, **Covered Jar,**
*2005. 23 ½ x 14 ¾ inches
(59.7 x 37.5 cm). Stoneware; salt glaze*

permit the slightly curving surface even one blank spot. At other times he uses stripes that, as they race across the plates and bowls, contrast with the shape that supports them. These delightful pieces provide the income that enables him to make more experimental as well as larger work. Vessels from his first kiln firing seem tame compared with a more recent piece (photo 43). The jar in photo 44, a Chinese-influenced shape, was fired on its side. Its height struggles with insistently horizontal bars of quickly flowing glaze and ash that capture a landscape of destruction and shadow beneath the flow. The colors gather and run; they are dense and explosive. Such an aesthetic appears impulsive but derives its power from the risks he takes.

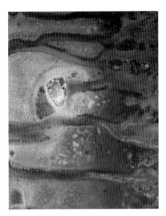

PHOTO 44:
DANIEL JOHNSTON,
Side-Stacked Vase, *2005.*
13 x 6½ inches (33 x 15.9 cm).
Stoneware; wood fired

PHOTO 43: DANIEL JOHNSTON, **Vase,** *2005.*
16 x 7½ inches (40.6 x 19 cm). Stoneware; wood fired

PHOTO 45: **Fred Johnston and Carol Gentithes,
Johnston and Gentithes Art Pottery**

Fred Johnston and Carol Gentithes

Both university graduates with advanced degrees, Fred Johnston and Carol Gentithes (photo 45) left their urban lives to live and make pottery in Seagrove, where they felt they could learn more and be part of a supportive environment. Carol Gentithes makes fantastic sculptures and decorates tiles that recall 17th- and 18th-century European ceramics. Carol says they also owe much of their energy to the seasonal landscape and its lively populace of cows, chickens, pigs, ducks, goats, frogs, and flying insects. Artists like Magritte, Chagall, and Picasso also inform her work (photo 46). Through the enamel emulsion that she uses for her decorations, she creates a colorful intensity that is possible only with this kind of glazing (photo 47). In some ways, her work is comparable to the painted and decorated wares of Bulldog and Dover potteries and LDDK Studios, because all have introduced very different formal ideas and decorative methods of work to the local traditions.

Johnston makes tableware that in its simplicity and wonderful colors recalls the Coles. Large lidded jars that could hold cookies are so engaging in their shape and decoration that their functionality hardly matters (photo 48). His teapots and pitchers, with their beaky spouts and bulbous bodies, are zoomorphic (photo 49). The surfaces of Johnston's work incorporates signs, markings, and drawings from both antique sources and contemporary art. Such diversity is also present when his shapes reference Mediterranean as well as Asian forms. The beaky spouts, for example, have ancestors on the island of Crete. The ostrich pot could be an umbrella stand or floor vase. Its strong ovoid shape draws on the local egg vase

PHOTO 46: CAROL GENTITHES, **Chagall Teapot,**
2005. 10½ x 8 x 10 inches, Porcelain; emulsion glazes

PHOTO 47: CAROL GENTITHES, **Watch Dog,** *2005.
10¾ x 17 x 11, Porcelain; emulsion glazes*

PHOTO 48: FRED JOHNSTON, **Blue Jar and Frogskin Jar,** *2005.*
13¼ x 11½ inches (33.7 x 29.2 cm); 11¼ x 12¼ inches (28.6 x 31.1 cm). Stoneware; salt glaze

form and that of ostrich eggs; the bird, elegantly composed on the belly of the pot, is stylized into line and shadow (photo 50).

Johnston's varied educational experience, constant reading and travel, and insistent curiosity about the process of making pots fuel his high-energy conversations. Whether he fires with a gas, an electric, or a nearly new wood kiln, Johnston experiments constantly.

PHOTO 49: FRED JOHNSTON, **Teapot,** *2005.*
6¼ x 10¾ x 5¼ inches (15.9 x 27.3 x 13.3 cm). Stoneware

PHOTO 50: FRED JOHNSTON, **Ostrich Pot,** *2005.*
22 x 14½ inches (55.9 x 36.8 cm). Stoneware

PHOTO 51: **Travis, Pamela and Vernon Owens, Jugtown Pottery**

Vernon and Pamela Owens

In contrast to the other work profiled here, that of Vernon and Pam Owens (photo 51) may seem conservative and traditional—but appearances deceive. The work they make is the result of a vision that grew with Vernon's development as a potter in his early years at Jugtown, a vision that he and his wife have shared since they bought the pottery in 1983. The Owenses' joint exploration of form and color continues as they make beautiful work with an elegant simplicity, modesty and confidence, much like the potters themselves.

Vernon's quiet sophistication and consummate skill is revealed in all the work he makes that plays riffs on Jugtown's own history. His Four-Handled Jar (photo 52), in the style of J. H. Owens, is a contemporary variation on the work of his grandfather (see photo 34, page 47) and the Persian jar that so defined the power of Jugtown's early potter, Ben Owen senior. This version is taller and thinner than either of the early forms could have dared to be. The combination of the wood-fired Cornwall and oxblood glazes is sparkling and powerful. The decoration, which plays such an important role in the early versions, is here obscured to the point that the emphasis is on the pure refined shape of the jar. It has the same defiant strength found in Stuempfle's work, or that of Ben Owen III; it is a jar for the ages.

The Owens couple also executes a wide variety of skillfully made useful ware. Vases, tableware, mugs, tumblers, and pitchers form the strong backbone of their shop's offerings. Some forms, like the candlesticks or Han vases, are deeply ingrained, having evolved out of the Busbee years, through Country Roads, and into the present. Other forms are new but related to earlier work and to other Asian forms. These have been refined, reconsidered, and renewed through experimentation with glazing and firing. The vase in photo 53, whose decorative bosses mark where the flared neck joins the globular base, is a familiar shape that could be trite, but in Pamela's

PHOTO 52: VERNON OWENS, **Four-Handled Jar in the style of J. H. Owens,** *2004. 22 x 14 inches (55.9 x 35.6 cm). Stoneware; Cornwall and oxblood glazes. Collection of Gallery of Art & Design, North Carolina State University, gift of artist, T2004.001.003*

PHOTO 53:
PAMELA OWENS,
Vase, *2004.*
14 x 8 ½ inches
(35.6 x 21.6 cm).
Stoneware; Chinese
blue glaze.
Collection of Gallery
of Art & Design,
North Carolina
State University,
gift of artist,
T2004.001.002

hands, her fluent marriage of glaze to shape epitomizes one of her perpetual concerns—the relationship of form to color. Her little teapots, mounted with silver lids and handles by her sister, Jennifer Lorette, epitomize the Owenses' awareness of the history of ceramics.

Following in Dot and Walter Auman's footsteps, Pam and Vernon created a pottery museum in 1988 that stands beside the shop that Juliana Busbee built. Filled with examples of early work

from the Seagrove area, the Owenses agree that it is a great source of inspiration. It is also a symbol of the unique circumstances that set them apart from many potters but join them to the other descendants of Seagrove potters. They live with Jugtown's history and its vision, and such experiences relate them to past and present in ways that are not accessible to younger makers trained elsewhere.

PHOTO 55: **David and Mary Farrell, Westmoore Pottery**

The Westmoore and Dover Potteries

The importance of adherence to a particular way of making pottery is also exemplified by the work of David and Mary Farrell at Westmoore Pottery (established in 1977), and Milly McCanless (photo 54), her former husband, Al, and their sons at Dover Pottery, opened in 1983. At that time, they joined the few potteries that were then in operation: Auman, Jugtown, Chriscoe, Teague and Melvin Owens.

David and Mary Farrell (photo 55) came to apprentice at Jugtown in the 1970s and stayed on to become solid members of the community. What the Farrells have given to the area is truly beautiful redware, faithful in many ways to the German and Pennsylvania work made by the Moravians in earlier centuries. It could hardly be more appropriate to see this work here; Bethabara and Salem are nearby and redware was the first pottery made there. The Farrells create a wide and varied selection of tableware decorated with stylized floral forms, dots, curvilinear strips, and bands of color, all made by slip trailing with a brush or squeeze bottle onto the bisqueware (photo 56). A clear glaze lets the strong red clay color show through while contrasting slip decorations emphasize shapes. We are connected to the work because it is so lively and beautiful. The charger made to celebrate the pottery's 20th anniversary is a tour de force (photo 57). Its crisp shape is informed by applied decoration that is controlled yet energetic.

The Farrells also make Bellarmine jars, jugs, and flasks in salt-glazed stoneware that are honest references to their origins in the useful ware of Germany. The Farrells' work wears well; it always feels fresh and new while its visual references to the past are comforting.

The McCanlesses moved to the area because of Al's job in Star but also because it seemed like a wonderful place to raise children. Milly first wanted to make hand-painted dollhouse miniatures, so she decided to study pottery making at Montgomery Tech. Al followed her, and his pharmacy background led him to glazes and the many

PHOTO 54: **From left: Eck, Milly, and Will McCanless, and Joe Cole, apprentice; Dover Pottery**

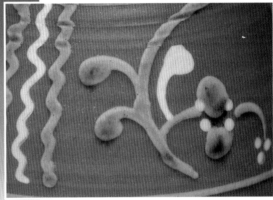

PHOTO 56:
WESTMOORE
POTTERY,
Redware Pitcher,
*2005. Height, 9 inches
(22.9 cm). Redware;
wheel thrown; slip-trail
decoration; electric fired
to cone 04*

PHOTO 57: WESTMOORE POTTERY, **Anniversary Charger,**
*1997. 4½ x 22 inches (11.4 x 55.9 cm) in diameter.
Redware; wheel thrown; sgraffito, slip-trail decoration;
electric fired to cone 04*

PHOTO 58: DOVER POTTERY, *Untitled, 1997.
1 x 11 ½ inches (2.5 x 29.2 cm) in diameter. Stoneware; pressed;
hand painted with Mason stain, copper carbonates by Milly
McCanless; electric fired to cone 3*

ways in which people had decorated wares. As Milly's skill and ability increased, she opened Dover Pottery in 1983. It was the 14th shop of its kind in the area. Some questioned whether Seagrove even needed another pottery. Others ridiculed or disdained her hand-painted porcelain ware (photo 58, page 113). Milly grew up with vividly painted Italian ware like that made by the potters of Deruta, and had developed an interest in Persian rugs. She and Al also liked Spanish, Italian, and Chinese painted wares. When, in addition to throwing ware, they started using jiggers and press molds to form work, some purists were offended. Although they were making pottery in traditional ways, Milly and Al were not making pottery in the Seagrove tradition.

Dover's colorful ware, decorated by Milly with rabbits, fish, and flowers, is comparable to work made by Denby Pottery in Massachusetts, or that by Deruta, an Italian maker, and also with Asian painted wares. Among the Seagrove pottery shops, Dover work has the greatest affinity with Westmoore pottery, though they employ a different clay body and different techniques for applying decoration. But the decorative technique at both potteries is dependent on intense, perfected, and refined hand and eye coordination. Some of the more elaborately decorated chargers (photo 59), made by Bruce Gholson and decorated by Will McCanless, are simply breathtaking.

Al McCanless started making crystalline-glazed vases about 1988. Phil Morgan had already been making crystalline in the Seagrove area for several years. (Walter B. Stephen first introduced crystalline ware to North Carolina when he opened his Pisgah Forest Pottery in Asheville, around 1926.) Crystalline work is for those who like the results of the process (photo 60). The iridescent patterns are like strange and mysterious flowers woven or embroidered on a transparent veil of color on the body of the pot. Between Milly's porcelain work and Al's crystalline ware, it must have seemed as if the McCanlesses were introducing foreign languages to the area. Their sons, Will and Eck, are now well trained, and their work holds the promise of continuing innovation of the inventive work of Dover Pottery (photo 61).

PHOTO 60: ECK MCCANLESS, *Untitled, 2005. 10¾ x 7¼ inches (cm) in diameter. Stoneware; wheel thrown; crystalline glaze; electric fired to cone 10.* COURTESY OF DOVER POTTERY

PHOTO 61: JOE COLE, *Untitled, 2004. 5¼ x 4¾ x 4¾ inches (13.3 x 12 x 12 cm). Stoneware; wheel thrown; incised; ash glaze; decoration by Will McCanless wood and salt fired to cone 12.* COURTESY OF DOVER POTTERY

Bulldog Pottery

Bruce Gholson and Samantha Henneke (photo 62) make unique pieces in series that can be functional or decorative, and are frequently both at once (photo 63) Their aesthetic is contemporary, American, and personal. The couple graduated from the esteemed ceramics program at the New York State College of Ceramics at Alfred University. Gholson worked at Dover Pottery and LDDK in the mid 1990s. In 1997, the two moved to the Seagrove area because the community valued pottery making.

They are constantly experimenting with shapes, glazes, and firing. In 2004, they made wall-mounted ceramic boxes that function rather like photographs or paintings. These were totally new to them and to Seagrove. The reason for their success is quickly apparent: the serpent on Snake Box is organic, the skin jewellike; it seems ready to slither off the surface and slide away (photo 64). Nature is captured, cultivated, and kept alive.

Gholson also makes crystalline ware whose attenuated porcelain forms and glazes seem to deny their material substance (photo 65). The surfaces glitter and reflect light—the glazes are so like glass, but these pieces take glass to a higher and different power of refraction and intensity.

Henneke and Gholson tend their garden and their land in response to the seasons. They are captivated by their adopted homeplace. They find inspiration for their work in the landscape, in arrowheads they find by the hundreds, in the insects that swarm in summer months, and in the imagined fossils of this verdant land (photo 66).

PHOTO 63: BULLDOG POTTERY, **Insect Boxes,** *2005.*
Tallest, 3¾ inches (9.5 cm). Porcelain, various glazes

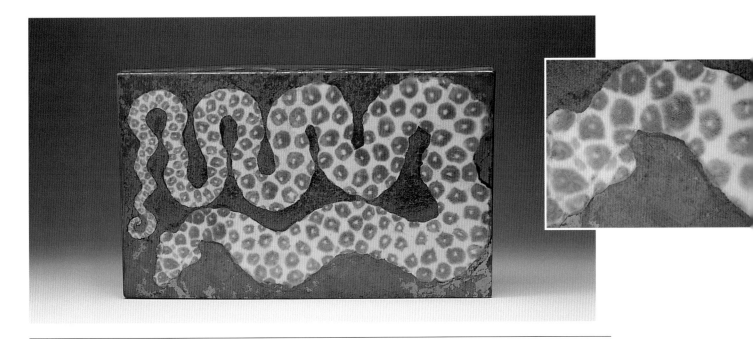

PHOTO 64: BULLDOG POTTERY, **Snake Box,** *2004. 18½ x 11 x 2 inches (47 x 27.9 x 5.1 cm). Porcelain; various glazes*

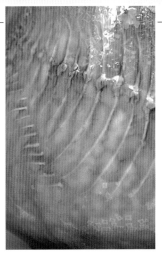

PHOTO 66: BRUCE GHOLSON, BULLDOG POTTERY, **Teapot with Fish,** *2002. 6½ x 8½ x 6 inches (16.5 x 21.6 x 15.2 cm). Porcelain; amber molybdenum crystalline glaze*

PHOTO 65: BULLDOG POTTERY, **Vases,** *2004. Left: 19½ x 5 inches (49.5 x 12.7 cm); center: 13½ x 4½ inches (34.3 x 11.4 cm); right: 25 x 7 inches (63.5 x 17.8 cm). Porcelain; crystalline glazes*

PHOTO 67: **Sid Luck, Luck's Ware**

Sid Luck

Up the road from Bulldog Pottery is Luck's Ware. Sid Luck (photo 67) came back to the area to take up the family tradition in the 1980s. He and his son Matt make wares based on the traditional forms of the area. Sid is a fine potter whose utilitarian pieces are straightforward, unassuming, honest, and strong. The pitcher shown in photo 68 typifies his production but for the fact that it is wood fired and salt glazed. For years, Luck said that he would never build a wood-fired kiln, but he couldn't resist the challenge. He and his two sons built theirs at the back end of his large shop. It is beautiful and the work that comes from it is too (photo 69).

Luck is as widely recognized for his teaching and mentoring of other potters as for his work (photo 70). It is tempting to think that this mirrors the past history of potting in the area. Luck's work and his success as a teacher are celebrated in an annual festival organized by many of his students. The students are essential to Seagrove's future. He has changed their lives by teaching them a skill that is personal, and will grow, change, and make them their own bosses. It is, his students say, a hard life and sometimes tenuous, but they would not change anything about it.

PHOTO 68: SID LUCK, **Pitcher,** 2005. 14¾ x 10¾ x 8¼ inches (37.5 x 27.3 x 21 cm). Stoneware; salt glaze

PHOTO 69: **Entry to wood-fired kiln at Luck's Ware.**

PHOTO 70: SID LUCK, **Teapot**, *2005. 7 x 9 x 9 inches (17.8 x 22.9 x 22.9 cm).*
Local clay; wheel thrown; salt glaze; wood fired in a groundhog kiln

POTTERS, POTS, AND PERSONALITIES

Understanding the chemistry that seems to pervade this amazing congregation of potters is not easy. It is tempting to see parallels between the potters' personalities and their work. One feels at times as if the essential goodness and gentle sweetness of the Farrells, for instance, are completely embodied in their redware, or that Fred Johnston's energy has spilled over into the polka dots that decorate some of his large vessels. Milly McCanless at Dover is gracious and ebullient; because of her love of pattern, her painted wares are displayed on antique furniture in rooms with Persian rugs. But Milly is also strong and opinionated about many issues, including feminism, pacifism, and the environment. Her work, then, only mirrors a part of her soul.

These makers are complex, talented, and, above all, private people. The work they show represents but a facet of the world in which they live. The work we see is the result of huge efforts and long years of questioning their personal visions and goals and of struggling to attain a satisfying standard. We never see what is thrown away. All of the Seagrove potters are driven by an individual ideal of perfection, to make nothing less than strong and consistent work. Some have goals that drive them perpetually to make new kinds of work, work that is sometimes vastly changed from what came before, sometimes only a few throws

speak to me in the voice that the potter has chosen. I don't always know if the clay is local or commercial, if the kiln is gas or wood, if the maker mixed her own glazes or not. Of course I usually am able to identify all these things, but first comes the voice of the work itself.

The ability of these people to elicit powerful feelings through their work is part of what makes me go back to the area again and again. Sometimes I need a new mug, sometimes a plate or a vase, and sometimes I just need to escape to a place that I know is not like where I live. Some of the potters' favorite stories are those that tell of the difference their work makes in the lives of those who use it. What more could one ask for than to know that the work of one's hands could cheer, comfort, amuse, and enrich a person's daily life?

TRADITION AND COMMUNITY PERSEVERE

A comforting mug, like a vase that holds flowers joyfully, represents more than an effort of making or a purpose fulfilled; they are solid reminders that you can return to the same place, to your house or your very own room, again and again. The natural world is constantly changing and can as easily destroy life as support it. It does not love us; we love it. So we make things: furniture, houses, clothing, and books to help contain and stabilize our constantly changing state as mortal beings. Most of us no longer can work with our

 CLAY IS THE SOURCE OF THEIR BEING. IT IS THEIR PASSION, THEIR PRIDE, THEIR OPPORTUNITY, AND THEIR CHALLENGE.

different from yesterday's jug. Of such progress, Pam Owens said, "we take baby steps," and I don't believe she means just small steps, but explorative, experimental ones, to find the best ways to make their wares (photo 71).

These potters consistently make work that speaks directly, without benefit of their makers' intervention. I walk into a shop and wait for the work to

hands to build our houses or make our clothes or furniture. Potters help us do this by giving us objects, things, that are unique, and become, through ownership, ours.

The strong ties that knit together farming families in rural 19th-century North Carolina have given way to movement. In the Seagrove area, some have stayed on the land, combining farming with commuting to jobs as barbers, teachers, store owners, shop keepers, sales personnel, and nurses. If the family farm could be held by one of the siblings, it frequently has become a locus for those who had left—a place to return to, much like the country church of family baptisms, marriages, or burials. Eventually, new residents found new communities, but the process of assimilation takes time and in the South it seems to take even longer.

The changes that have moved across this region of the mid South have come even more slowly to the somewhat isolated Seagrove area, because its farms and incomes have been modest. The potters who were able to adapt and develop their production continued more or less uninterrupted in the old way of life that is embedded in a wider farming community, its churches and schools. Such cir-

cumstances provide a layer of continuity and tradition that is not the same as that afforded by the clay, the abundance of wood, water, and the like. The native potters have a relationship to making pottery that is rooted in the work and the place that is quite unlike that of the academically trained studio potters who have moved there. And their connection to making ceramics is different from those who have learned to make pottery as a way to free themselves from unsatisfactory jobs or no jobs at all.

Seagrove's farming life has shaped all the area's natives and bestowed upon them a realm of reality that interprets continuity and tradition differently from more recent residents. Whether potter or farmer, their realm is more deeply in touch with the tenuous and uncertain qualities of life.

PHOTO 71: PAMELA AND VERNON OWENS, **Low Wide Vase, Vase with Lip,** *and* **Vase,** *2004.*
Left: 4 ½ x 6 inches (11.4 x 15.2 cm); center: 7 ½ x 8 inches (19 x 20.3 cm); right: 9 ½ x 7 inches (24.1 x 17.8 cm).
Stoneware; copper glaze; wood fired; color variations from same firing due to kiln placement

Surface clay in Randolph County, near Seagrove.

Farmers never forget what a terrible drought can mean. There is a harsh edge to such a reality, a toughness, a resilience, and a confidence that cannot be learned. It cannot be understood easily, or even well articulated. It springs from the memories of hunger, work, holidays, and mealtimes. Southern writers have delved for decades into these habits of life and mind, which are filled with contradictions and fears, consistencies and joys. Potters who grew up in the Seagrove area share in a common life that is not part of the life of the newly arrived. Such disparate experiences are revealed in the way in which the potters perceive their work and how they live in a community.

and persistence. Sometimes the potters appear to each other as being radically different from themselves, and irritating, without worthy values or purposes to share. Yet there is admiration, honesty, humor, openness, warmth, ease, and delight in the success of others; at times, an almost reckless joy in the business of being a potter and doing so in Seagrove. There is also jealousy, deceit, anger, contempt, and stress—and the desire that the newer people would simply leave. In such a climate, generational and familial differences are sometimes magnified. The Christian parable of the workers who begin in the morning, those who come at noon, and those who come very late plays in my mind when I think of Seagrove. We are told that all the workers should be paid the same (and are welcomed to the Kingdom of God), but it took me decades to learn that the parable is about compassion and acceptance, not income. I also believe the Seagrove community experiences the contradictions that go with a job one does because one can and must do it, so different from the view that pottery is a deeply creative undertaking that is as dependent on talent as training. To some makers, throwing ware must seem as ordinary and quotidian as breathing, but others have to work very hard to learn the skill. Yet those who can throw never seem to lose the skill, even if they have to leave it for a while.

The work goes on at all times, and what significantly sets this place apart is that for all its potters, potting is a way of life. Making wares informs all

THE WORK GOES ON AT ALL TIMES, AND WHAT SIGNIFICANTLY SETS THIS PLACE APART IS THAT FOR ALL ITS POTTERS, POTTING IS A WAY OF LIFE.

It would seem that there are two communities in Seagrove: the old and the new. But such a categorical distinction cannot adequately describe life there. What is more accurate is that there are many communities—each pottery is almost its own society. And they all thrive together, sometimes connecting directly through their expertise and practice with clay, sharing the values of hard work

that they do, and the work unites them with their physical world on a day-to-day basis that is unimaginable for most of us. Everything affects the work—not only the health and energy of the potters themselves but also the seasons, the humidity, the heat, the cold, the rain, the snow. More than one potter talks about the differences that can occur in a firing based on the weather, which he or she sometimes learned only through bitter experience.

And it is more than the weather; it is the continuous contact with a substance that can be as recalcitrant and stubborn as an angry child, as malleable as sweet, soft butter, as personal as a smile. Potters have laughed at the texture of a clay or thrown it angrily to the ground. Whether it comes in a box or from one's own pugmill, clay is the source of their being. It is their passion, their pride, their opportunity, and their challenge. And it puts their lives in their own hands.

These potters, these atoms dancing on the strings of Highway 705 and Seagrove's many country roads, exist together in an era of abundance where there are few constraints to guide, define, or shape the work that they produce—nothing except the limits suggested by the traditions of the community, the public that buys, the potters who teach, their dreams and visions of singular pieces. Keeping in mind that Seagrove is a crazy quilt of old and new, local and not, rural and urban, is the only way to even begin to appreciate the work that is made there now. More than likely, this web of potters and their families will preserve it for the future because we continue to buy their pots—because we can, because we want to, because they are made by real people, and because they are objects made by human hands. Pots represent stability in a natural world that has no regard for humans and a human world that changes from moment to moment. The same coffee mug each morning is a comfort. Thousands of coffee mugs leave Seagrove every year, along with many other pieces of pottery. More than that, each body of work by a pottery studio fills a different niche and a different need, regardless of the actual function embodied in a pitcher, a bowl, or a vase.

All this activity is now supported by the recent ascendance of American craft, which has made Seagrove what some potters are calling a "little Japan." It suggests that there is great respect for the potters and their work, and that work is supported by a large number of buyers. The resurgence of interest in wood firing, the annual potters' conferences in Randolph County that bring national and international figures to the area, and increased exposure and access to the work and the potters through Internet websites

have all contributed to the belief that the Seagrove area is a great place to live and create and sell work. It is almost as if Seagrove itself has become intrinsically valuable, a cultural icon that endows its potters with a particular cachet as sweet as the status that is sometimes acquired by attending certain craft schools or workshops.

Jack Troy, a contemporary potter, has written admiringly of Seagrove and its traditions, noting that nowhere else is wood firing "better integrated" into daily life and work. He has called Seagrove the U.S. equivalent of France's La Borne. I would amend his compliments to say simply that nowhere is the craft of making pottery better integrated into daily life than in the Seagrove area, where both its history and current practice infuse its practitioners with the hope and the confidence that they will continue to succeed and make pottery for another hundred years.

MILLY McCANLESS, **Dinner Plate,**
circa 2004. 9½ inches in diameter (24.1 cm)
Porcelain; various glazes

90 Potters,
15 Miles:
A Snapshot

A LITTLE MOORE POTTERY
Chrissy Little and Glenda Little
1140 S. Hwy 705
Seagrove NC

Many of the artistic clay creations of Glenda Little, Chrissy's mother, are one-of-a-kind pottery pieces. Glenda graduated from Pembroke State University and taught art in schools in Randolph and Moore counties. Chrissy graduated from East Carolina University majoring in Fine Arts with a concentration in ceramics. A Little Moore Pottery opened in 2002.

ALBRIGHT POTTERY
Arllie Albright
6597 New Center Church Road
Seagrove NC

ANITA'S POTTERY AND
DOGWOOD GALLERY
Anita Morgan
2513 Hwy 705
Seagrove NC

AVERY POTTERY AND TILEWORKS
Blaine Avery and Laura Avery
1423 Hwy 705
Seagrove NC

Avery Pottery and Tileworks is housed in a renovated 1800s log cabin, and offers a selection of contemporary pottery and tile with traditional themes and a modern flair.
WWW.DISCOVERSEAGROVE.COM

BLUE MOON GALLERY
Byron and Georgia Knight
1387 Hwy 705
Seagrove NC

BMG offers one of the largest and most diverse selections of traditional and contemporary pottery, featuring locally, regionally and nationally known artists in the state of NC.
WWW.BLUE-MOON-GALLERY.COM

BLUE STONE POTTERY
Audrey Valone
2215 Fork Creek Mill Road
Seagrove NC

A. R. BRITT POTTERY
Aaron Britt
5650 US Hwy 220 South
Asheboro NC

Turning and producing pots for 16 years in the Seagrove area by maintaining and continuing the traditional style of pottery taught to me by Nell Cole Graves.
WWW.SEAGROVEPOTTERY.NET

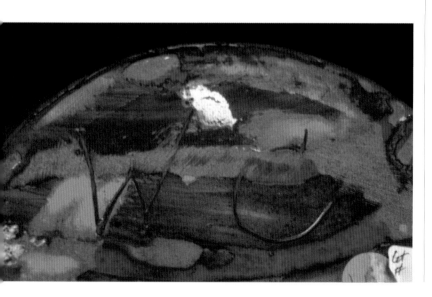

BROOKE HAVEN
Melanie M. Dennison
209 East Main Street
Seagrove NC

The most dynamic hand-built stoneware available, featuring vessels of elegant form and function with vibrant glaze hues in violet, blue, and copper-red reduction.

BULLDOG POTTERY
Bruce Gholson and Samantha Henneke
3306 US Hwy 220 North
Seagrove NC

A pottery studio exploring creative ideas through fine craftsmanship. We make beautiful, individual art pieces tempered by classical sensibilities to adorn your office, home, or table.
WWW.BULLDOGPOTTERY.COM

CADY CLAY WORKS
John Mellage and Beth Gore
3883 Busbee Road
Seagrove NC

John's elegant forms are accented with rustic patterns from the path of the flame in the wood kiln or layers of Beth's richly colored glazes.
WWW.CADYCLAYWORKS.COM

CAGLE ROAD POTTERY
Gordon Ray, Pat Ray, Paul Ray, and
  Patrick Rowe
603 Cagle Road
Seagrove NC

Cagle Road is a family-owned and operated business. Our traditional forms are made on a potter's wheel. Some are hand painted with North Carolina themes (lighthouses, roosters, wildflowers). Others are fired with a single or combination of glazes.

CALLICUTT POTTERY
Gary Callicutt
5137 Seagrove Plank Road
Asheboro NC

Gary and Rosa Callicutt opened Callicutt Pottery in 1999. They do mostly functional pieces such as coffee mugs, soup mugs, apple bakers, pie pans, corn-bread pans, plates, bowls of many sizes, and much, much more.

GRAHAM CHRISCOE POTTERY
Graham Chriscoe
2719 US 220 North
Seagrove NC

CHRISCOE'S POTTERY
Mack Chriscoe
1360 South Hwy 705
Seagrove NC

Chriscoe's Pottery is a one-man pottery shop that opened in 1982. The potter believes in producing a well-turned, useable and pleasing to look at pot.

CLAY POND POTTERY
Alan Long
109 Burney Road
Asheboro NC

Sixth-generation pottery featuring traditional, functional wares and very decorative specialty pottery and sculptures. Apprenticed with Sid Luck (wife's cousin).

COUNTRY POTS
Michael Moore
2035 Hwy 705 South
Seagrove NC

Direct descendant of Teague Potters. Large selection of shapes and colors. Oven, dishwasher, and microwave-safe kitchen items. Some decorative pieces.

CRAVEN POTTERY
Donna Craven
2616 Old Cox Road
Asheboro NC

All pieces are wood fired and salt glazed, although I use some slips and ash glazes. Mostly traditional, functional; also includes decorative and carved wares.

CROSS CREEK POTTERY
Terry and Vivian Hunt
481 King Road
Seagrove NC

Cross Creek Pottery is committed to producing high-quality original pots at an affordable price. Ranging from the utilitarian to the decorative, pots are done in salt-glazed and glazed ware. We believe in usefulness without sacrificing style.

DEAN–MARTIN POTTERY
Stephanie Martin and Jeff Dean
7739 Nathan Lane
Seagrove NC

Bright, colorful stoneware; contemporary shapes; wheel thrown and slab built.

DIRT WORKS
Dan Triece
1226 Hwy 705
Seagrove NC

Dirt Works Pottery is a customer-friendly, diverse gallery and working pottery shop producing contemporary functional and decorative pots to enhance everyday lives. Dirt Works pottery is in private collections worldwide.

DIXIELAND POTTERY
Randy James and Sherry James
1162 Cagle Loop Road
Seagrove NC

Dixieland Pottery was established in 1988 and we are from pottery families. We make highly crafted work and focus on the natural beauty of the clay.

DOVER POTTERY
Will, Eck, and Milly McCanless, and Joe Cole
321 Dover Pottery Drive
Seagrove NC

Dover Pottery is a family-run business established in 1983. It is one of the oldest functioning potteries in the area and specializes in zinc silicate, crystalline glazes, hand-painted majolica, and wood-fired salt glaze. Dover operates out of a log barn on a scenic farm in the historic Westmoore community.

DOWN HOME POTTERY
Michael Dunn
888 Chrisco Road
Seagrove NC

FAT BEAGLE POTTERY
Charles "Doc" Tostoe
677 Potters Way Road
Seagrove NC

With over 20 years' experience, I produce a standard glaze ware line, a wood ash line, a cobalt blue–textured matte line, raku, and a pit-fired line. Pottery is not just a job, it's a lifestyle.
WWW.CCLAY.COM/FATBEAGLE/INDEX.HTM

FIRE SHADOW POTTERY
Sally Larson and Mo McKenzie
244 Falls Drive
Eagle Springs NC

Inspired blends of form and glaze create one-of-a-kind treasures. Clay transformed into natural elegance for your home. Visit Sally and Mo at Fireshadow Pottery.
WWW.FIRESHADOW.COM

FORK CREEK MILL POTTERY
Ann Williams
246 Old Plank Road
Seagrove NC

As a versatile potter, Ann Williams uses different firing techniques to make pottery that combines skills of 30 years with sparks of creativity and bits of feline inspiration.
WWW.SEAGROVEPOTTERIES.COM

FREEMAN POTTERY
Judy Freeman-Foushee
1147 McDuffie Road
Eagle Springs NC

Freeman Pottery produces hand-turned miniatures in a variety of shapes and glazes. Their sgraffito-designed functional pottery features trees, fences, barns, churches, log cabins, and "Johnny houses". The shop is located in a scenic family farmhouse.

FROM THE GROUND UP
Michael Mahan
172 Crestwood Road
Robbins NC

Breathing new life into an ancient craft, Michael Mahan creates many varieties of pottery, including horsehair pots, soul pots, meditation bells, and tableware using a wood-fired burnishing technique.

TOM GRAY POTTERY
Tom Gray
1480 Fork Creek Mill Road
Seagrove NC
WWW.N2CLAY.COM

GREAT WHITE OAK GALLERY
Benjamin Burns and Bonnie Frazier
437 N. Broad Street
Seagrove NC

HICKORY HILL POTTERY
Daniel Marley and Leanna Marley
4539 Busbee Road
Seagrove NC

Hickory Hill Pottery was established in 1985 in the Westmoore community. Our goal is to continue the tradition of the area by producing wares commonly found here for years.

HOLLY HILL POTTERY
Richard Gillson
625 Fork Creek Mill Road
Seagrove NC

JAKE'S POTTERY
2132 Hwy 705
Seagrove NC

JOHNSTON AND GENTITHES ART POTTERY
Fred Johnston and Carol Gentithes
249 Main Street
Seagrove NC

The work of Johnston and Gentithes draws inspiration from many cultures, mythologies, and life's observations. Johnston is best known for his wood-fired, zoomorphic pottery while Gentithes is best known for her quixotic sculptures.
WWW.JOHNSTONANDGENTITHES.COM

JUGTOWN POTTERY
Vernon Owens, Pam Owens, Lara Stewart, and Travis Owens
330 Jugtown Road
Seagrove NC

Jugtown Pottery, listed in the National Register of Historic Places, continues a tradition of pottery excellence. The Sales Cabin has Jugtown Pottery and American crafts; museum.
WWW.JUGTOWNWARE.COM

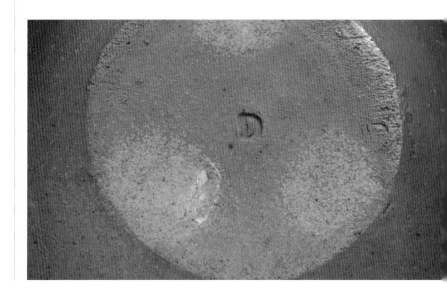

CRYSTAL KING POTTERY AND FOLK ART
Crystal King, Anna King, and Terry King
2233 Garren Town Road
Asheboro NC

One of Seagrove's most interesting shops for Southern folk art and colorful functional ware. Third-generation pottery with a wide selection of face jugs, and whimsical figures in animal, political, and biblical themes.

E. J. KING POTTERY
Evin J. King
649 Dawson Miller Road
Asheboro NC

The Pottery Shop is located on South Highway 705, Seagrove, across from Westmoore School and Jake's Pottery Shop.

KINGS POTTERY
Terry King, Anna King, and Crystal King
4905 Reeder Road
Seagrove NC

Here at Kings Pottery we carry on a 200-year-old tradition of producing hand-turned traditional stoneware, wood-fired salt glazes, and folk pottery that has been passed on through family history.
WWW.KINGSPOTTERY.COM

KOVACK POTTERY
Craig Kovack
1298 Fork Creek Mill Road
Seagrove NC

Kovack Pottery is a marriage between the potter and the artist. Each piece is hand-turned and then hand-painted with floral and other patterns.
WWW.KOVACKPOTTERY.POTTERYGROVEGIFTS.COM

LANTERN HILL
Kitt Vanderwahl
6725 Old US 220
Seagrove NC

LATHAM'S POTTERY
Bruce and Janice Latham
7297 US Hwy 220 South
Asheboro NC

Hand-turned stoneware, functional and traditional, with colors in cobalt blue, burgundy, purple, green array of spongeware and old-looking glazes all microwave and dishwasher safe.
WWW.DISCOVERSEAGROVE.COM

LDDK POTTERY
Linda Dixon and Drew Krouse
PO Box 446
Seagrove NC

LION'S DEN POTTERY
Bobbie Brewer
PO Box 229
Seagrove NC

LUCK'S WARE
Sid Luck, Matt Luck, and Jason Luck
1606 Adams Road
Seagrove NC

Fifth-generation potter (Matt and Jason are the sixth). We try to carry on the forms of our ancestors.

LUFKIN POTTERY
Sally Lufkin Saylor
PO Box 468
Seagrove NC

I specialize in jewel-tone glazes on pottery you can use in your home, such as dinnerware, porch pieces, and accessories.

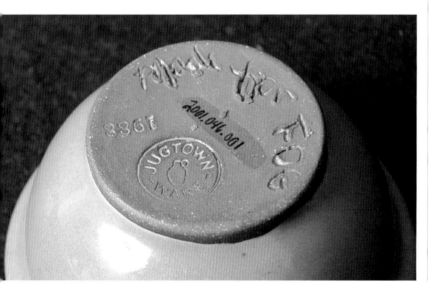

CHRIS LUTHER POTTERY
Chris Luther
4823 Busbee Road
Seagrove NC

Coming from the Chriscoe pottery family of Seagrove, North Carolina. Chris expands on tradition by exploring innovative shapes, textures and colors. Visit his newly opened showroom.
WWW.CHRISLUTHERPOTTERY.COM

MAGNOLIA PLACE
Barbara Voncannon
PO Box 460
Seagrove NC

JACK MANESS
Jack Maness
1914 Gray Owl Road
Asheboro NC

MARSH POTTERY
Bobby Marsh
1497 Cagle Loop Road
Seagrove NC

McNEILL'S POTTERY
Windy Wallace, Roger Wallace, and
 Garrett McNeill
1208 Upper Road
Seagrove NC

A family business; they have about 20 different glazes and do a line of snow people, with a different one every year.

MOORE POTS POTTERY
Larry Moore
333 Jugtown Road
Seagrove NC

PHIL MORGAN POTTERY
Phil Morgan
966 Hwy 705
Seagrove NC

A Seagrove native, Phil Morgan established his pottery in 1973, producing the finest in crystalline-glazed porcelain and salt-glazed stoneware. Visitors are welcome anytime.
WWW.SEAGROVEPOTTERIES.COM

MY TURN POTTERY
Rhonda Myrick
220 Willie Road
Seagrove NC

NEW SALEM POTTERY
Hal Pugh and Eleanor Minnock-Pugh
789 New Salem Road
Randleman NC

Located on the site of the William Dennis Pottery (circa 1790); New Salem Pottery continues the tradition of slip-decorated and plain redware.
WWW.NEWSALEMPOTTERY.COM

NICHOLS POTTERY
Garry Nichols, Tommy Nichols,
and Rebecca Nichols
128 Williams Drive
Eagle Springs NC

Opened in 1994 as a small family business. We strive to provide our customers with the best quality while maintaining great prices. All pots are signed "God Bless You."
WWW.POTTERYVILLE.COM

OLD GAP POTTERY
Philip Pollett
944 Hwy 705 S
Seagrove NC

OLD HARD TIMES POTTERY
John McNeill, Janey McNeill, Daniel Johnston,
 and Chad Brown
7672 Union Grove Church Road
Seagrove NC

Traditional-style pottery; salt-glazed stoneware and decorative, along with a friendly, down-home, country atmosphere.

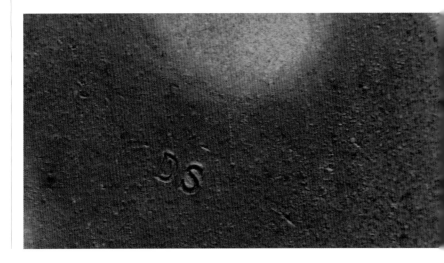

OLD HOUSE POTTERY
Fred Beane
Hwy 705, 236 Beane Lane
Seagrove NC

OLIVE BRANCH POTTERY
Janis Van Der Staak
236 Old Plank Road
Seagrove NC

Specializing in custom designs and personalized pottery and handmade custom tiles.
WWW.SEAGROVEPOTTERIES.COM

O'QUINN'S POTTERY
Sandra O'Quinn and Glenn McNeil
4456 Busbee Road
Seagrove NC

Located in a quaint 100-year-old home, O'Quinn Pottery specializes in functional, salt, and self-mixed glazes in several variegated color schemes, as well as unique larger decorative pieces.

BEN OWEN POTTERY
Ben Owen III
2199 Hwy 705 South
Seagrove NC

Specializing in quality wood-fired stoneware and earthenware. Ben Owen III continues a family tradition of beautifully turning functional and decorative pieces with a contemporary touch.
WWW.BENOWENPOTTERY.COM

ORIGINAL OWENS' POTTERY
Boyd Owens
3728 Busbee Road
Seagrove NC

PEBBLES POTTERY
Pebbles Bryson
7127 Hwy 705
Eagle Springs NC

My shop is in a little old house my grandmother grew up in. Most of my work is functional, but I also do decorative pieces such as North Carolina vases, dogwoods, and hand-carved items. All glazes are lead free.

PINEY WOODS POTTERY
Johnnie and Georgia Maness, Judy King, and
   Phyllis Cagle
1430 Ether Road
Star NC

Beginning on the wheel and finished by hand, Piney Woods Pottery's clay creations are unique three-dimensional pieces that include flower varieties and even animals.

POT LUCK POTTERY
Laura Teague Moore
1830 South NC Hwy 705
Seagrove NC

POTTERY JUNCTION
Regina Vonncannon
325 W. Main Street
Seagrove NC

POTTERY SHOPPE IN SEAGROVE
Bobbie Listerman and Suzie Smith
476 N. Broad Street
Seagrove NC

POTTS POTTERY
Jeff and Linda Potts
630 E. Main Street
Seagrove NC

Linda came from nine generations: Sheltons, Kings, and Coles. The love of pottery and joy of turning was the incentive to open our own shop. Our satisfaction comes from making a useful piece with rich glazes that brings everyday pleasure.
WWW.POTTSPOTTERY.COM

RAVEN POTTERY
Anne Raven Jorgensen
PO Box 411
Seagrove NC

Functional pottery in a variety of contemporary colors, shapes, and designs

RAY POTTERY
Paul Ray and Sheila Allred
460 Cagle Road
Seagrove NC

At Ray Pottery we produce quality pottery, both functional and decorative. Pots are designed to have both visual and tactile appeal.

CHARLES RIGGS POTTERY
Charles Riggs
462 Firetower Road
Carthage NC

ROCK HOUSE POTTERY
Ken Poole
1792 South NC Hwy 705
Seagrove NC

SEAGROVE POTTERY
Gene King
106 N. Broad Street
Seagrove NC

Gallery with more than 60 local potters. We feature local pottery, sculpture, glass, basketry, and jewelry. Our locations are adorned with candles, wool hats, scarves, stained glass, and much more.

SCOTT'S POTTERY
Tina Scott
143 Jugtown Road
Seagrove NC

SHELTON'S POTTERY
Mitchell Shelton
391 Cagle Road
Seagrove NC

STACY'S POTTERY
Stacy Lambert
3531 Kemp Mill Road
Asheboro NC

Studied under Sid Luck since 1993. Full-time cotton mill employee, self taught in pottery, great side job, can't make the stuff fast enough. Chances are I'll do this until the day I die.
WWW.RTMC.NET/~ODDWERKS.COM

STUEMPFLE POTTERY
David Stuempfle
1224 Dover Church Road
Seagrove NC

Expressive shapes, natural surfaces, and wood-fired, local clays. Available daily at LDDK Pottery, Main Street, Seagrove.
WWW.STUEMPFLEPOTTERY.COM

SUNSET POTTERY
Harold Stutts
123 Sunset Drive
Robbins NC

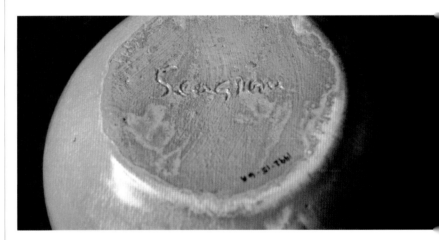

A. TEAGUE POTTERY
Archie Teague
2132 Hwy 705
Seagrove NC

TURN AND BURN POTTERY
David Garner and Deborah Garner
PO Box 371
Seagrove NC

VERNON POTTERY
Calvin Hogue Vernon
1066 Chrisco Road
Seagrove NC

*Established in 1994 by Calvin Hogue Vernon, a
Caswell County, North Carolina, native. Vernon
Pottery sells a small but select variety of functional,
well-thrown ceramic shapes.*

**VILLAGE POTTERY MARKETPLACE
OF SEAGROVE**
Melanie M. Dennison
205 East Main Street
Seagrove NC

*Seagrove's largest gallery, featuring top-quality
works from more than 100 local and regional potters
and fine craftsmen.*

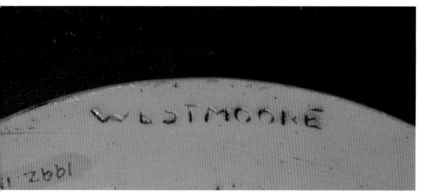

WALTON'S POTTERY
Don Walton and Susan Walton
326 Adams Road
Seagrove NC

WESTMOORE POTTERY
Dave Farrell and Mary Farrell
4622 Busbee Road
Seagrove NC

*Westmoore Pottery specializes in historical pottery of
styles made and used in North Carolina in the 17th,
18th, and early 19th centuries. Many historical sites
and historical movies use our replica work because of
its accuracy.*
WWW.WESTMOOREPOTTERY.COM

WHYNOT POTTERY
Mark Heywood and Meredith Heywood
1013 Fork Creek Mill Road
Seagrove NC

*Whynot Pottery is known for its rich gas-fired ware.
Potters Mark and Meredith Heywood have operated
their pottery since 1982. They work mainly in
stoneware fired to just over 2300 degrees. They make
production pottery, but you will always find them
working on something new and different.*
WWW.WHYNOTPOTTERY.COM

WILLIAMS POTTERY
Sharon and Tony Williams
2170 Dan Road
Robbins NC

*I do functional stoneware. The pottery in my shop
ranges from flowing multi-color glaze to a matte
hand-painted finish, decorative and functional.*

WYNDHAM POTTERY
Wyndham Dennison
209 East Main Street
Seagrove NC

*Hand-turned stoneware and porcelain art-pottery
collectible vessels in reduction fire with unique one-
of-a-kind contemporary glazes.*

BIBLIOGRAPHY

Auman, Dorothy, and Charles G. Zug III. "Nine Generations of Potters: The Cole Family," *Southern Exposure* 5, no. 203 (1977): 166–79.

Beam, Bill, Jason Harpe, Scott Smith, and David Springs. *Two Centuries of Potters: A Catawba Valley Tradition*. Lincolnton, NC: Lincoln County Historical Association, 1999.

Bishir, Catherine W., Charlotte V. Brown, Carl R. Lounsbury, and Ernest H. Wood, III. *Architects and Builders in North Carolina: A History of the Practice of Building*. Chapel Hill: University of North Carolina Press, 1990.

Bishir, Catherine W., and Michael T. Southern. *A Guide to the Historic Architecture of Piedmont North Carolina*. Chapel Hill: University of North Carolina Press, 2003.

Bivins, John F. Jr. *The Moravian Potters in North Carolina*. Chapel Hill: University of North Carolina Press, 1972.

Blumer, Thomas J. *Catawba Clay: Pottery from the Catawba Nation*. Exhibit catalog. Seagrove, NC: North Carolina Pottery Center, 2000.

Brunk, Robert S. ed. *May We All Remember Well: A Journal of the History and Cultures of Western North Carolina*, 2 vols. Asheville, NC: R. S. Brunk Auction Services, 1997, 2001.

Burrison, John A. *Brothers in Clay: The Story of Georgia Folk Pottery*. Athens: University of Georgia Press, 1983.

Busbee, Jacques. "Jugtown Pottery: Its Origin and Development—An Intimate Touch of the Local Color That Is Molded into this Historic American Ware." *Ceramic Age* 14, no. 4 (October 1929): 127–30.

Busbee, Juliana R. "A New Way for Old Jugs." *Bulletin of the American Ceramic Society*, October 1937.

Clark, Ivan Stowe. "An Isolated Industry: Pottery of North Carolina." *Journal of Geography* (September 1926): unpaginated.

Craig, James H. *The Arts and Crafts in North Carolina, 1699–1840*. Winston-Salem, N.C.: Old Salem, Inc. 1965.

BEN OWEN III, **Oribe Vase**. *2005. 11½ x 6½ inches (29.2 x 16.5 cm). Wood-fired porcelain*

Crawford, Jean. *Jugtown Pottery: History and Design.* Winston-Salem, N.C.: John F. Blair, 1964.

DeNatale, Douglas, Jane Przybysz, and Jill R. Severn. *New Ways for Old Jugs: Traditions and Innovations at the Jugtown Pottery.* Exhibit catalog. Columbia, S. C,: McKissick Museum, 1994.

Dietz, Ulysses G. *The Newark Museum Collection of American Art Pottery.* Newark, New Jersey: Peregrine Smith/Newark Museum, 1984.

Eaton, Allen H. *Handicrafts of the Southern Highlands.* New York: Russell Sage Foundation, 1937.

Fries, Adelaide L., ed. *Records of the Moravians in North Carolina: Volume I, 1752–1792.* Raleigh, NC: Edwards and Broughton, 1922.

_____. *Records of the Moravians in North Carolina: Volume 5, 1784–1792.* Raleigh, NC: North Carolina Historical Commission, 1941.

Greer, Georgeanna H. *American Stonewares: The Art and Craft of Utilitarian Potters,* Exton, PA: Schiffer Publishing, 1981.

Hertzman, Gay Mahaffey. *Jugtown Pottery: The Busbee Vision.* Exhibit catalog. Raleigh: North Carolina Museum of Art, 1984.

Hewitt, Mark, and Nancy Sweezy. *The Potter's Eye, Art & Tradition in North Carolina Pottery.* Exhibit catalog, North Carolina Museum of Art. Chapel Hill: University of North Carolina Press, 2005.

Huffman, Allen, and Barry G. Huffman. *Innovations in Clay: Catawba Valley Pottery.* Exhibit catalog. Hickory, NC: Hickory Museum of Art, 1987.

Huffman, Barry G. *Catawba Clay: Contemporary Southern Face Jug Makers.* Hickory, NC: A. W. Huffman, 1997.

James, A. Everette. *North Carolina Art Pottery, 1900–1960: Identification Value Guide.* Paducah, KY: Collector Books, 2003.

Johnson, Bruce E. "Built without an Architect: Architectural Inspiration for the Grove Park Inn," in Brunk, *May We All Remember Well,* I: 214–27.

Johnson, Pat H. "O. L. Bachelder: Omar Khayyam Pottery," *Pottery Collectors Newsletter* 1, no.11 (August 1972): 144–48.

Johnson, Pat H., and Daisy Wade Bridges. *O. L. Bachelder and His Omar Khayyam Pottery.* Exhibit catalog. Charlotte, NC: Mint Museum of Art, 1984.

Jordan, James C. III, and Jane Ellen Starnes, curators. *Southern Arts and Crafts, 1890–1940.* Exhibit catalog. Charlotte, NC: Mint Museum of Art, 1996.

Leftwich, Rodney. *From Mountain Clay: The Folk Pottery Traditions of Buncombe County.* Cullowhee, NC: Western Carolina University, 1989.

Juliana Busbee, to Harvey K. Littleton May 27, 1957, Harvey K. Littleton Papers, Gift of Harvey K. Littleton, Smithsonian Institution.

Lock, Robert C., with Yvonne Hancock Teague, Archie Teague, and Kit Wanderwal. *The Traditional Potters of Seagrove, North Carolina and Surrounding Areas from the 1800s to the Present.* Greensboro, NC: Antiques and Collectibles Press, 1994.

Morton, W. D. *Handmade: A History of the North State Pottery Company 1924–59.* Boonville, NC: Carolina Avenue Press, 2003.

Outlaw, Alain C. "Preliminary Excavations at the Mount Shepherd Pottery Site," *The Conference on Historic Site Archaeology Papers,* 1974, edited by Stanley South, 2–12, Columbia: Institute of Archaeology and Anthropology, University of South Carolina, 1975.

Pugh, Hal. "The Southern Friend," *Journal of the North Carolina Friends Historical Society* 10, no. 2 (Autumn 1988): 1–26.

Rauschenberg, Bradford L. "Andrew Duché: A Potter 'a Little Too Much Addicted to Politicks,'" *Journal of Early Southern Decorative Arts* 10, no. 1 (1984): 14–74.

Scarborough, Quincy. *North Carolina Decorated Stoneware: The Webster School of Folk Potters.* Fayetteville, NC: Scarborough Press, 1986.

_____. *The Craven Family of Southern Folk Potters: North Carolina, Georgia, Tennessee, Arkansas and Missouri.* Fayetteville, NC: Quincy Scarborough Companies, 2005.

Scarborough, Quincy, and Robert Armfield. *The Walter and Dorothy Auman Legacy.* Fayetteville, NC: Quincy Scarborough Companies, 1992.

Schwartz, Stuart C. "The Royal Crown Pottery and Porcelain Company, Merry Oaks, North Carolina," *Pottery Collectors Newsletter* 3, no. 5 (February 1974): 57–62.

Smith, Howard. *Index of Southern Potters: An Alphabetical Index of 18th, 19th and 20th Century Potters Encompassing the States of North Carolina, South Carolina, Georgia, Alabama, and Mississippi.* Mayodan, NC: Old America Company, 1982.

South, Stanley. "The Ceramic Ware of the Potter Rudolph Christ at Bethabara and Salem, North Carolina, 1786–1821," *Conference on Historic State Archaeology Papers,* 1968, pt.1 (August 1970): 33–52.

Spangler, Meredith Riggs. "In Prayse of Potts," *Potters of North Carolina,* edited by Margery W. Adams, 2: 5–23. Charlotte, NC: Ceramic Circle of Charlotte, 1973.

Sweezy, Nancy. *Raised in Clay: The Southern Pottery Tradition.* Washington, DC: Smithsonian Institution Press/Office of Folklife Programs, 1982.

Taylor, Terry B. "Sunset Mountain Pottery," in Brunk, *May We All Remember Well, I*: 50–62.

Whatley, L. McKay. "The Mount Shepherd Pottery: Correlating Archaeology and History." *Journal of Early Southern Decorative Arts* 6, no 1 (1980): 21–37.

BRUCE GHOLSON,
Toad Pot, *2004.*
9¼ x 13¼
x 13¼ inches
(23.5 x 33.7
x 33.7 cm).
Porcelain

_____. *The Architectural History of Randolph County, North Carolina.* Asheboro, NC: City of Asheboro, the County of Randolph, and the North Carolina Division of Archives and History with assistance from the Randolph County Historical Society and the Randolph County Arts Guild,1985.

Wilkinson, Joe. "Clay Crafters" and "Glaze Master: The C. R. Auman Pottery and Charles B. Masten." Manuscripts for "North Carolina Potter Masters: C. R. Auman and C. B. Masten," exhibit at the Gallery of Art & Design, North Carolina State University, Raleigh, April 2001.

Zug III, Charles G. *Turners and Burners: The Folk Potters of North Carolina.* Chapel Hill, NC: University of North Carolina Press, 1986.

RELATED WEBSITES

HTTP://WWW.AAA.SI.EDU. (ARCHIVES OF AMERICAN ART)
HTTP://WWW.ANCESTRY.COM (CENSUS RECORDS)
HTTP://WWW.CENSUS.GOV (US CENSUS RECORDS AND DATA)
HTTP://WWW.LOC.GOV
HTTP://WWW.CS.UNCA.EDU/NFSNC/RECREATION/UWHARRIE/
HTTP://WWW.DISCOVERSEAGROVE.COM
HTTP://WWW.HOMEOFGOLF.COM
HTTP://WWW.MONTGOMERY-COUNTY.COM
HTTP://WWW.MOOREHISTORY.COM
HTTP://WWW.NCPOTTERYCENTER.COM
HTTP://WWW.THEPOTTERIES.ORG
HTTP://WWW.TUFTSARCHIVES.ORG
HTTP://WWW.VISITRANDOLPH.ORG

ACKNOWLEDGMENTS

Although the growth of information about the Seagrove area potters is discussed in my narrative, it is essential to acknowledge some particular works. Charles G. Zug III's *Turners and Burners: The Folk Potters of North Carolina* (UNC Press, 1986) and Nancy Sweezy's *Raised in Clay* (Smithsonian, 1984) are solid scholarly documents, and I could not have written without their perspectives and without the documentation they have presented.

Museum exhibitions have also played a major role in understanding the potters. Zug's exhibition, *The Traditional Potters of North Carolina*, at the Ackland Art Museum in 1981, and Gay Mahaffey Hertzman's *Jugtown Pottery: The Busbee Vision*, an exhibition at the North Carolina Museum of Art in 1984, examined different aspects of the Seagrove story. In 1987, the Gallery of Art & Design's *Vernacular Pottery of North Carolina* chose ceramics made by 20 potters based on Sweezy's study; 13 were from the Seagrove area. Following this exhibition, Phyllis Blair Clark curated another exhibition for the Gallery, called *North Carolina Clay*, in 1992. She included the work of 71 traditional and studio potters, and the Seagrove area was represented by the same potters who had been included in the 1987 exhibition.

The contextual relationship of pottery making was examined in the McKissick Museum's 1994 exhibition, *New Ways for Old Jugs*. This show, held in Columbia, South Carolina, considered Jugtown and its founders from the perspectives of the Arts and Crafts Movement, the Colonial Revival, and the appearance of modernism in America. *Southern Arts and Crafts: 1890–1940* at Charlotte's Mint Museum, in 1996, traced similar relationships among some of the individuals and organizations who shaped early 20th-century crafts.

That period in craft history has also gained by the recovery of many related stories. The C. R. Auman Pottery and its potters has been one of the most fascinating discoveries, pieced together by Joe Wilkinson, Billy Ray Hussey, Stanley Hicks, and others. Joe Wilkinson was inspired by Dorothy Auman, who first told him of the mysterious glaze master who had worked for C. R. Auman. *North Carolina Clay Masters: C. R. Auman and C. B. Masten*, a 2001 exhibition at the GAD, curated by Joe Wilkinson, showed 160 pieces made by the Auman pottery. It became evident that the Auman Pottery's ceramics could easily stand alongside those of Jugtown, the J. B. Cole Pottery, and the art pottery of western North Carolina.

No matter how many books are written, however, the pottery remains an inescapable fact that no approach can completely explain. The pots themselves are intransigent bearers of meaning, but

Face pitchers and mugs on the window sill in Fred Johnston's and Carol Gentithes' shop.

they are not silent. Some have more to say than others, many say the same things, some say little or nothing, and a few give us odes, poems, and prophecies. And we can try to give voice to those meanings. Talking about what objects mean is the result of a cumulative process that depends on people as well as the pots, and it starts with looking—countless hours of looking and the willingness to know you will always miss something. I owe immense debts to Arthur Baer, Sid Baines, Jen Bireline, Joseph and Pamela Briggs, Kathy Brown, Steve Compton, Leon Danielson, Tom and Cindy Edwards, Mark Hewitt, Barry and Allen Huffman, Billy Ray Hussey, Bill Ivey, Everette James, Bobby and Claudia Kadis, Charles Millard, the late W. D. Morton, George Viall, George Williams, Joe Wilkinson, and the late Ray Wilkinson, all of whom have shaped and reshaped my understanding and my appreciation for the immense body of work produced by the Seagrove-area potters.

I owe a similar debt to all the potters I have talked to in the past two years. Unfailingly gracious and generous with their time, the potters I interviewed contributed to this publication in many different ways. I have visited many of the potteries in the area and although I sometimes introduced myself as a person studying pottery, mostly I just walked in like any other visitor. That way I could look and touch and ask questions without feeling self-conscious or like some kind of expert from out of town. The potters whose work I discuss represent the diversity of experiences, traditions, and meanings that I found in the area. The potters who responded to my written survey were especially helpful, as was Jenny Lorette, whose access to the Seagrove Area Potters Association membership list has enabled us to include an up-to-date presentation of who is working in Seagrove as of the publication date.

I have also been helped by my colleagues, Catherine Bishir, Abie Harris, Barry Huffman, Andrew Glasgow, Denny Mecham, Barbara Perry, and Terry Zug, who listened as I tried to explain myself. Bethel N. Thompson's personal memoir of visiting the Seagrove area for nearly 40 years was also informative. Cynthia Bringle and Michael Cindric read portions of the manuscript for accuracy about the processes themselves and I thank them. I would also like to thank George Howard, who generously loaned me early-19th-century maps for me to study; one of these appears both on the cover and on pages 6 and 7.

Perhaps the greatest influence has been the collection at North Carolina State University's Gallery of Art & Design, where I work. The North Carolina ware alone numbers about 1,000 pieces. Thus, I have been privileged to spend many hours with the work. Whenever possible, I have described and illustrated work

from the collection because I believe deeply that a long and repeated association with objects provides an education about form and meaning that can be acquired no other way. Not all the pots at the GAD are the very best examples of work by one potter or another but all the pottery is part of the story.

I must also acknowledge Robert S. Brunk and Brian McCarthy, who suggested to Lark Books that I write this book. Special thanks are due to ceramics editor Suzanne Tourtillott. When she and I visited the Seagrove area in early February 2005, I think she caught something of the place and that, along with all her other direction, has been invaluable. Nathalie Mornu, associate editor, who assembled the images from my lists, was unfailingly patient. The book's designer, Dana Irwin, expanded my ideas of what the book might be like and then enabled those ideas to be realized.

I also eagerly thank the entire staff at the Gallery of Art & Design of North Carolina State University. Their help, patience, knowledge, and skills have supported me like a family. Gregory Tyler, registrar, and John Williams, her assistant, have played critical roles with regard to documentation and imaging. Timothy Ayers, who photographed the work, is also extremely knowledgeable about pottery, and he and I have talked for hours, good hours. And finally, I would like to thank my son, Jonathan Vestal Brown, who knows he has a pottery-mad mother, my friends Martha B. Ashby, Susan Arrendell, and Charles McMurray, who traveled with me to Seagrove, and my cousins, Tom and Cindy Edwards, who encouraged me to do this book because of our mutual love for the pottery.

ABOUT THE AUTHOR

Charlotte Vestal Brown, who grew up in Chatham County, North Carolina, became the Curator of Art at North Carolina State University in 1982, and has served as the founding director of the Gallery of Art & Design since 1992. She received her PhD in the History of Art at the University of North Carolina in Chapel Hill, where she was twice named a Kress Foundation Fellow. Brown served as assistant curator at the North Carolina Museum of Art, then held the position of assistant professor at Duke University until 1979. She is a contributing author to Houghton Mifflin's *The Humanities: Cultural Roots and Continuities*, first published in 1979 and now in its seventh edition. Brown was project director and a contributing author to the prize-winning *Architects and Builders in North Carolina: A History of the Practice of Building* (UNC Press, 1990) and was consultant for *A History of the North Carolina Chapter of the American Institute of Architects* (David Jackson, 1998). For her contributions to architectural history and to the profession, she was awarded honorary membership in the American Institute of Architects in 2002.

Brown has built a design and decorative arts collection at NCSU that includes historical as well as contemporary objects, and which focuses on American accomplishments and connections abroad. She has organized over 50 exhibitions and publications at the Gallery, including *The New Narrative: Contemporary Fiber Art* (1992), *Bob Trotman: A Retrospective* (1994), *Mark Hewitt, Potter* (1997) *The New Heritage of North Carolina Pottery* (2000) and *The Jewelry of Robert Ebendorf: A Retrospective of Forty Years* (2003).

INDEX